COOS COOPERATIVE

3 2881 00401

P9-CKF-733

649

LANSKY

Lansky, Vicki
Toilet training

DATE DUE			
AP 20 '94			
FE 15 '96			
JE 25 '97			
JE 26 '97			
JA 04 '00			
OC 11 '01			
FEB - 3 2009			

A

Rev.

M BOOKS

NEW YO   LONDON•SYDNEY•AUCKLAND

Thanks to Editors:
Toni Burbank, Maria Mack, Kathryn Ring, Sandra Whelan, Jeane-Marie Sohlden, Kate Moore and Carol Lowry.

Consultants:
Karen Olness, M.D., Minneapolis Children's Health Center
Judy Owens-Stively, M.D., Minneapolis Children's HealthCenter
Peggy Osterholm, R.N., P.N.P., Wayzata Children's Clinic
Rebecca Kajander, R.N., P.N.P., Wayzata Children's Clinic
Burton White, Ph.D., Center for Parent Education, Newton, MA
Joan Reivich, Booth Maternity Center, Philadelphia, PA
Meg Zweiback, R.N., P.N.P, M.P.H., Oakland, CA
Daniel P. Kohen, M.D., Minneapolis Children's Health Center

Illustrator: Jack Lindstorm

Special thanks to the parents who shared their words and feelings. Their quotes are reprinted with permission from Vicki Lansky's *Practical Parenting*™ *Newsletter* and respondents toVicki Lansky's Practical Parenting column in *Sesame Street Magazine Parents' Guide.*

THE FAR SIDE COPYRIGHT ©1986 UNIVERSAL PRESS SYNDICATE. Reprinted with permission. All rights reserved.

TOILET TRAINING
Nine printings in previous editions
Revised edition/ May 1993
All rights reserved.
Copyright © 1984, 1993 Vicki Lansky
Cover photo copyright © 1984 by Bill Cadge.

No part of this book may be reproduced or transmitted in any form or by any means, electronic or mechanical, including photocopying, recording, or by any information storage and retrival system, without permission in writing from the publisher. For information address: Bantam Books.

Library of Congress Cataloging-in-Publication Data
Lansky, Vicki
Toilet training : a practical guide to daytime and nighttime training / Vicki Lansky. — Rev. and updated.
p. cm.
Includes index.
ISBN 0-553-37140-1
1. Toilet training. I. Title.
HQ770.5.L36 1993
649' .62—dc20
92-35022
CIP

Published simultaneously in the United States and Canada

Bantam Books are published by Bantam Books, a division of Bantam Doubleday Dell Publishing Group, Inc. Its trademark, consisting of the words "Bantam Books" and the portrayal of a rooster is Registered in U. S. Patent and Trademark Office and in other countries. Marca Registrada. Bantam Book, Inc., 666 Fifth Ave, New York, New York 10103.

PRINTED IN THE UNITED STATES OF AMERICA
0 9 8 7 6 5 4 3 2 1

CONTENTS

Why Is Toilet Training Such a Big Deal?

❧

A number of things can contribute to a parent's strong need to get a child toilet trained, *right now*. Some are pressures from your peers, fear that you're failing as a parent by tolerating a child in diapers, the enrollment of your child in nursery school, and, not least, the strains and stresses of what's known as "diaper drag."

First, assume that any neighbor or relative who claims victory in toilet training her child before yours is lying (well, maybe exagerating), fantasizing, or redefining the term. I never considered my children really trained until they could get in and out of the bathroom, get their clothes off and back on, clean their bottoms properly, and wash their hands all without any help from me. But for now, we'll work with that more limited but still important definition that simply has the child saying, "Get me to the potty" in time.

Second, plan not to take it personally. Your child's readiness for toilet training is no indication of his or her IQ, your level of parenting ability, or your parents' attempts to raise you properly. *(Despite what your mother-in-law might say, your 3-year-old still being in diapers will not affect her social status.)*

Third, be assured that it *will* happen. When your child is truly ready, physically and emotionally, toilet training will happen rapidly. And be assured also that while it's going on, toilet training is very, very important, but when it's accomplished, you'll wonder why it seemed like such a big deal!

Fourth, remember that you are not alone. When your child regresses for the third time, meditate on the fact that, simultaneously, several million other mothers and fathers are earning their toilet-training merit badges, too.

Perhaps the biggest controversy on this subject today is the language used to describe the process. It's called "toilet learning," "potty training," "toilet teaching," and "toileting." Yes, *learning* may be more accurate than *training,* at least according to today's wisdom, but I've never had anyone ask me if my child was toilet learned. So please bear with my preference for toilet training, and don't search for deeper meanings.

Remember that there are three things
you can never make your child do—
eat, sleep, or go to the bathroom.

Chapter 1

When Is My Child Ready to Be Toilet Trained?

❧

The days of hand-hemmed, hand-washed, line-dried diapers are gone, thank goodness. So that should signal an era of more relaxed, less anxious parents, right?

Wrong!

The prospect of toilet training today evokes as much concern as it ever did. The pressures of friends and relatives—even doctors—as well as practical considerations have pushed many parents into premature toilet-training attempts that eventually ended in failure and frustration.

It is true that current wisdom has made many parents less intense about having a child trained before the age of 2. Early training is no longer the norm, but once a parent decides that the time has come, relaxation seems to go out the window.

The simple fact is that your child must be physically and emotionally mature enough to understand and to control what is happening in the process. If you begin to toilet train a child before this point, the odds are that it simply won't work. A child who is "trained" before age 2 usually has a toilet trained parent—one who is trained to catch the child!

Physical maturation first becomes possible with voluntary control over the sphincter muscles—which means being able to open and close very specific internal muscles. While this is possible by about 1½ years, this voluntary control only truly begins when a child can distinguish the sensations that precede a bowel movement or urination. This, in turn, depends on a certain amount of maturity of the central nervous system, over which no one has control.

> **You don't toilet train children—you wait for their bodies to mature (a fact God has already worked out). I made a game of it, with a timer set for 15 minutes after drinking a liquid. My son loved it!**
> *Linda Hurstell, Vicksburg, MS*

Emotional readiness is also crucial. A child's sense of self starts to emerge around the age of 2. For the first time, the child realizes that he or she can affect the world and his or her own life. Unfortunately, one of the first manifestations of this newfound power is the terrible twos stage, during which the child seems interested only in affecting his or her world negatively! It's not all bad, though. One of the positive results of this emerging assertiveness is a desire to grow up. And one of the best examples of grown-up behavior a child can relate to is being toilet trained. Once your child arrives at this point, he or she is more likely to cooperate with your toilet training efforts because he or she wants to. Body mastery is more self-rewarding than a desire to please.

The *average* child cannot be successfully toilet trained before the age of about 28 months. While girls are often trained by 2, boys may not be trained before 3 or later. But of course the exception to prove this rule will inevitably be your neighbor's child, a child in your child's play group, or your sister-in-law's child.

Whether a child is placed on a potty seat at 6 weeks, 6 months, or 16 months, most children will not be reliable until after the age of 2.

And no two children, even siblings who have been treated in exactly the same way, will be ready at the same age. There is a right time to begin this process, but it varies from child to child. Any time before the age of 4 is normal, despite what Grandma (or anyone else) says.

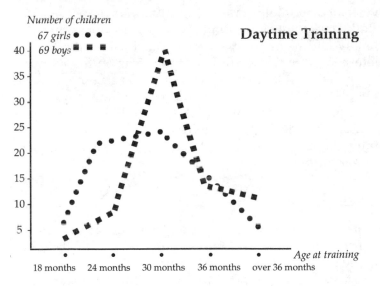

Daytime Training

Number of children
67 girls ● ● ●
69 boys ■ ■ ■

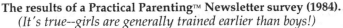

The results of a Practical Parenting™ Newsletter survey (1984).
(It's true--girls are generally trained earlier than boys!)

You might wish to consider the advantages and disadvantages of early toilet training before making a decision to try it. By early, I mean from age 1 to 2.

Advantages of Early Toilet Training

The advantages of early toilet training are obvious. In fact, they're the same as the advantages for toilet training in general, you just get to enjoy them sooner. Parents are anxious to have their children trained for a variety of reasons. Caring for an untrained child takes more planning and a lot of equipment. Travel and baby-sitting are more cumbersome. Wet diapers can cause diaper rash. (One mother told me her daughter trained herself in one day to escape a particularly painful case of diaper rash.)

On the average, dealing with diapers consumes approximately ten hours a week for most parents. A year's worth of disposable diapers is costly, as is a diaper service. Cloth diapers that you launder yourself are not as cheap as they would seem at first, when you consider the cost of detergent, electricity, and wear and tear on the laundry equipment, not to mention Mom and Dad. Some nursery schools won't take children in diapers, or they may charge more for the inconvenience. All in all, life is a lot more pleasant and less complicated when diapers become a thing of the past. And the attitude of most parents is "the sooner the better."

Just as we were finished toilet training our son, our next child (a girl) started wanting to use the toilet. She would watch her brother sit on the toilet and cry to take her diaper off. I fought her for three weeks, refusing to potty train two at once. But finally I thought if she was that insistent, she was ready. I put her in training pants, and three weeks later (at 18 months) she was completely trained.

Charlotte Martin, Bartlesville, OK

Disadvantages of Trying to Toilet Train Too Early

However nice it is to finally have a toilet-trained child, the process shouldn't *(and usually can't)* be rushed. Consider these disadvantages which are a high price to pay for a lowered cost of diapers:

- Trying to toilet train a child who isn't ready can prove to be futile and a waste of time.

- A child who is forced to try to comply may experience an extreme sense of failure (and so may the parents!).

- Premature toilet training may create a war of wills in which no one wins. A child may actually hold back bowel movements, creating serious constipation problems in an attempt to control the parent.

- The stresses of futile attempts at training may cause a parent to use inappropriate regimentation or force. Studies show that one of the principal causes of child abuse is parental frustration over a child's unsuccessful toilet training.

- A child's anxiety about toilet training may lead to bedwetting into adulthood. (A study of 18-year-old British army inductees provided a classic example of this. Fifteen percent were still bed-wetters after having been toilet trained before the age of one.)

We know that early rigid and coercive tactics are not worth the success they might achieve. In fact, rigid and coercive tactics used later in the training process can ALSO create more problems than they solve!

While most professionals today advocate later-is-just-fine, Katie Van Pelt in her book, *Potty Training Your Baby* (Avery Publishing), stands alone believing you should begin training before your child's first birthday.

I have been at odds with my 4-year-old for more than two years. We seem to backslide a lot (sort of like two steps forward, one step back). I think I put too much pressure on him in the beginning. We are trying to be more laid back with our younger child.

Becky Wilkins, Lubbock, TX

As one who did not get trained until age 4½ myself, I would not suggest the issue first. Once either of ours decided he or she wanted to use the potty and wear panties, that was the key.

Jodi Junge, Huntingdon Valley, PA

What Are the Basics?

You'll probably think about toilet training long before you get into it. One thing you'll want to do is settle any major differences of opinion between you and your spouse (or anyone else who will be involved) about methods and ways of handling things. Some compromise may be called for, because basic consistency is very important. But there should be total agreement that there's no place for punishment in any phase of toilet training.

General Signs of Readiness

From the time your child is about 2 (though it may be nearer 3 for some), you should watch for signs of readiness for training. If certain signs are clearly present, and the child is basically past the negative "no-to-every-request" stage, he or she is probably ready.

You'll know your child is ready when he or she:

- Is aware of the "need to go," and shows it by facial expression or by telling you.

- Can express and understand one-word statements, including such words as "wet," "dry," "potty," and "go."

- Demonstrates imitative behavior.

- Dislikes wet or dirty diapers. (*Don't confuse this with your level of discomfort or inconvenience.*)

- Is able to stay dry for at least two hours or wakes up dry after a nap.

- Is able to pull elastic waist pants up and down.

- Is anxious to please you.

- Has a sense of social "appropriateness" (wet pants can be an embarassment).

- Tells you he or she is about to go. (Praise such statements to set the stage for a child who wishes to please you by learning to use the toilet or potty.)

- Asks to use the potty chair or adult toilet!

Check Fluid Intake

If your child shows all the signs of readiness except the ability to stay dry for at least two hours, check fluid intake. Any child who is drinking milk, water, or fruit juices continuously cannot stay dry for long. Also, check with your doctor about the possibility of a lactose intolerance (the inability to digest milk properly) which can result in cramps, loose stools and the inability to hold a bowel movement for more than a moment.

Some Preparatory Steps

There is much to be said for setting the stage well before you begin toilet training. Few children train themselves. They need to know what's expected of them! They need and deserve your help and guidance. A child who has become familiar with bathroom procedures and equipment is more likely to become trained quickly and easily than one who has not.

- Take your child into the bathroom with you. It's especially helpful if fathers and brothers set the example for boys, and mothers and sisters set the example for girls. Siblings are often pleased to act as role models. If your privacy is important to you, don't forget that there are neighborhood children who would probably be delighted to demonstrate. Today's experience with outside-the-home day-care often lets children "learn" from their peers and often speeds up their learning curve.

- Try to help your child recognize the sensations of "being wet," "wetting now," and "about to be wet." Encourage your child to talk about these sensations—especially "about to be . . ." sensations—without pressing your child to be toilet trained. Comment on signs you notice, such as the child's pausing in play or walking as if he or she is uncomfortable after elimination. Use statements such as, *"You are having a BM,"* rather than asking the general question, *"What are you doing?"* Asking your child to let you know when the diaper is wet or messy is another way of increasing awareness.

- Let your child go nude in appropriate settings to help the child "see" what he or she is doing, and to help make the mental connection between the words and what they refer to.

- Changing a diaper in the bathroom will also associate the process with the place. Children over age 2 should be off the changing table for this reason.

- Although much ado has been made about using the proper terminology for body parts and functions, you should use the words that come most easily to you and your child. "Peeing," for example, may be more effective than the term "urinating" if the latter is a forced term. DO use specific terms, though; "going to the bathroom" is too vague. Try not to use words that will make your child think of his or her bodily functions as being dirty or disgusting (for example, "dirty," "stinky," "yucky," etc.).

- Help your child learn the meaning of the terms "before"

11

and "after" by using them yourself in other contexts such as, *"We'll wash the dishes after dinner."*

- Talk about the advantages of being trained: no more diaper rash, no more interruptions for diaper changing, the pleasure of being clean and dry. Discuss training as an important stage of growing up.

- Let your child practice lowering and raising training pants sometimes, or putting them on and taking them off.

- Have a potty chair handy on which the child may sit (even with clothes on) perhaps while you are in the bathroom yourself, but only if he or she wants to. The intent is not to get results, but to provide familiarity with the equipment. And let the child flush the toilet for you, to help him or her get used to the noise it makes and avoid possible fear later on.

- Begin reading "potty" books to your child. Many good ones are available. (See pages 55–59.)

I don't think there's any one way to toilet train children. They can be tempted, coaxed, yelled at or put on the potty every hour, but they won't really be trained until they decide they're ready.
Marlene Gwiazdon, Osceola, WI

Nothing I try has worked. My 3-year-old understands everything about potty training, but tells me, "I'm not ready, Mommy." So I try not to say anything. If he's not ready, he's not ready.
Kyle Lutz, Mill Valley, CA

Chapter 2

Should I Choose a Potty Chair, an Adapter, or the Toilet Seat?

Some experts claim that we complicate the toilet training process when we require children to learn on several different kinds of equipment in succession. We start them on the potty chair, then move them to the adapter seat, and finally, we move them to the adult toilet—making three tasks for them to learn.

There is much to be said for using one, two, or all three of these methods. I suspect that the choice really isn't all that significant. Your choice will depend on your child's size, age, and preference; your preference (*which I think counts for a lot*); and the size and number of your bathrooms. Whatever method you settle on will probably work just fine for you and your child.

Potty Chairs

Proponents of the potty chair say it allows a child to be more independent, since a parent doesn't need to lift the child to the toilet. It also allows a child to place his or her feet squarely on the floor when bearing down to eliminate, and the child can also use the support of the chair arms. Because a potty chair is obviously the child's own, he or she will take pride in possessing it.

I know many parents like the flexibility of the potty chair, moving it to various rooms in the house to suit their convenience, and using it for travel as well. (Others claim that a potty chair should remain in the bathroom, so its purpose becomes solely associated with the bathroom.)

If you have a potty in the bathroom, you and your child can go to the toilet at the same time.

One disadvantage is that a boy will not be able to urinate standing up—it will be too difficult to aim, and there will be too much splashing. Another consideration is that it needs to be cleaned out by you or your child. In the beginning, cleaning out the pot will be fun. With experience, it loses its appeal for a child—and probably for you too.

If the potty chair appeals to you, you should get one before you start training so it becomes a familiar piece of equipment to your child. In fact, you may even let your child shop for the chair with you. You can narrow the choice down to two or three styles, and let your child choose from among those. This can make the child all the more anxious to try it out.

Personalizing a potty chair or adapter will also make it more unique and interesting. You can do this by adding a few stickers or decals of your child's choosing. Or use press-type letters and spell out your child's name.

Let your child know that it's okay—for now—to sit on the potty with clothes on to get used to it, but when he or she is ready, it will be used as *"Mommy and Daddy use the toilet."* Avoid using the seat at other times so as not to confuse the issue.

Choosing a Potty Chair

If you opt for a potty chair, you will probably choose a miniature version of an adult toilet, a molded one-piece style chair a child straddles or a plastic molded stool-type chair. Many potty chairs today convert to adult toilet seat adapters as well.

- Before purchasing a potty chair, check to see how the pot is removed. If the pot is hard to get out or it has to be tipped, don't buy it.

- If you want a urine deflector, look for a removable one made of flexible plastic. Potties with deflectors seem to be easier to find than those without them, but if your child is hurt by one when trying to seat himself, he may refuse to use the seat.

- Buy a floor model that won't slide around and is stable.

- Consider buying more than one potty chair, especially if you have more than one bathroom or a two story house. The extra one can always be used for car travel or left at grandma's.

- Be aware that if you get a potty chair with a tray, lifting it up will be one more step your child will have to master.

- Look into the possibility of buying an adult camping portable potty for a child who's unusually large.

Cleanup Responsibility

- Make cleaning the potty chair chamber easier by keeping an inch or so of water in the bottom of the pot.

- Or place a few sheets of toilet paper on the bottom for a quicker clean-up of bowel movements.

- NEVER put any bleach in the bottom of a clean chamber pot. Urine contains ammonia and if a child urinates into the bleach it will cause a chemical reaction producing toxic fumes. Using bleach to disinfect the pot in the cleaning process, however, will not be problematic.

- Consider having your child be responsible for cleanup. Not every parent is comfortable with this, nor will every child adapt to it. Keep in mind that it's not really developmentally appropriate for a very young child.

- Fascination with feces is not unique to your toddler. To prevent a child from playing with it, take the potty chamber out of reach after use. You may need to wait a bit before flushing it if your child is insistent. This stage usually does not last too long. *Whew!*

Potty training is a lot like a first kiss. You can't do much about it—it just happens. In my daughter's case, potty training occurred over a weekend. The key, found out by accident, was that she didn't want to be taken to her potty and prompted (*how silly of me to think that that would work!*) but rather, characteristically, wanted to do it herself. Once we got that straight, all I had to do was praise the results.

Kathe Grooms, St. Paul, MN

Popular Commercial Potty Chairs

Listed on this and the following pages are just some of the potty chairs you will have available to you from manufacturers. They are representative of what is available. Most stores tend to carry one to three styles. Many styles convert from floor models to use as toilet seat adapters. You can always call a store first to see whose brands they carry (and the price) or you can contact the manufacturer's customer service department (see listing for manufacturers' addresses and phone numbers on page 106) and they can possibly direct you to an outlet in your area.

Many of today's potty seats are made by companies that also specialize in toys. Their plastic injection molding techniques have been transferred to other juvenile products, such as potty chairs.

This *Saddle Potty* (*Playskool Baby*) of molded plastic sits stably on the floor. Suggested retail price under $8.

The *Portable Potty* (*Biobottoms*) is available in pink, blue, and white plastic. It's lightweight but sits solidly on the floor. Suggested retail price under $15.

The *DooDah Potty* (*Innovative Distributing*) is a white, molded, music-activated potty using two camera batteries. A waterproof-sealed computer chip starts the music(*OldMacDonald*)when used. Suggested retail price under $16.

The **Potty Chair** (*Baby Bjorn*) is a molded floor potty with a white, lift-out potty chamber fitted with a splash guard. It has a high back though they also make a low back, one piece model. It is made in Sweden. Suggested retail price under $38.

This molded plastic **Potty** (*Fisher-Price*) has a dark blue base and a white molded top that lifts off to act as an adapter on an adult toilet seat. Suggested retail price under $20.

Here is a molded, one piece **Potty Seat** (*Little Tikes*) which has a wide, stable base with skid-resistant rubber feet. There is a fold-down seat lid. There is a convenient carrying handle in the back. Suggested retail price under $12.

This molded plastic **Perfect Potty** (*Evenflo*) begins as a floor model with a removable pot. The seat top can be removed and used on an adult toilet, but it also folds in half for travel convenience. The base becomes a step stool or portable seat. Suggested retail price under $20.

Tot's 1st Choice Potty Seat (Safety 1st) is dark blue molded plastic, with bright red and green easy-grip handles, that starts as a floor model with a yellow pot chamber. The removable top transfers to the adult toilet. Suggested retail price under $16.

The *Toilette Plus Trainer (Cosco)* is a 3-stage seat that begins as a floor model, has a seat with a lid that detaches to fit an adult toilet, and a base that can then be flipped and used as a step stool, with the adapter or the direct use of the toilet. Suggested retail price under $26.

This folding, hardwood *Nursery Chair (Nu-Line)* comes with and without the attached tray. The plastic white seat has a removable pot chamber. Suggested retail price under $12.

Here is a decorative, hand-painted solid wood **Potty Chair** *(Shades of Jade)* of attractive cut outs. Available designs are a bunny, zebra, a train and one with balloons. Suggested retail price under $75.

The **2-Way Potty Trainer** *(Century)* is a plastic commode-style potty seat. The chamber is removed from the rear. It has a hinged lid, and the top lifts off to fit an adult toilet seat. Suggested retail price under $18.

The *Gerry Potty Seat (Gerry Baby Products)* has a front removable pot chamber, a tilt-down deflector that allows the lid to close and a detachable top seat that snaps onto an adult toilet. Suggested retail price under $14.

The **Let's Potty! Trainer** *(Sassy)* has a low-to-the-floor design. Remove the pot, fold the legs under, and it converts to a toilet top adapter. It's designed for use with disposable bags. Suggested retail price under $18.

The white **2-Stage Trainer Toilet** *(Gerry)* is a 2-in-1 potty chair/step-up training seat to use as an adapter It converts from a floor seat to adult toilet use with a built-in ladder/footstool. Suggested retail price under $20.

Choosing an Adult Toilet Adapter Seat

Many of today's toilet top adapters come from the multi-use floor models. But they can be purchased singly also. They come as seats, molded rings (some of which fold up) and as stepladder adapters, all to reduce the opening of adult toilet seats for small size bottoms.

Adapters are lightweight and portable and have the additional advantage of direct flushing, so there is no extra cleanup necessary. However, adapter seats can be a nuisance for the rest of the family if there is only one bathroom and the adapter is in the way and must constantly be removed and replaced in innovative ways. Some styles have tried to overcome that complaint.

Many of these seats come with vinyl straps implying that a child is left alone on the seat and needs extra safety protection. In the early stages of training, a child should not be left alone. No child should be strapped in place and then left! That is likely to feel like punishment to a child. Stay with your child. If you haven't gotten the desired results within three to five minutes, you aren't going to. As children take on the responsibility of using the toilet with an adapter, they will be on and off by themselves in no time, and the strap is unnecessary.

You may wish to consider buying an inflatable or folding adapter seat for use when traveling (see *Traveling During Training*, page 75) or shopping, regardless of the method you opt for at home.

This **Padded Potty Seat** *(Mommy's Helper)* is a vinyl, padded ring that sits atop the toilet. It fits all standard toilet seats and is easy to remove. Suggested retail price under $14.

The **Pelican Potty Seat** (*Pelican Co*) is a molded adapter ring that fits under any toilet seat. The adult seat closes down on it, holding it firmly in place. The top and bottom deflector shield has a low profile. Suggested retail price under $8.

This white plastic **Toidy Seat** (*Baby Motivations*) also fits on the toilet, held in place under the ring of the adult toilet. It fits all standard and elongated seats and comes with a non-detachable deflector. It can double as a bath tub safety seat for a toddler. Suggested retail price under $22.

The **Trainer Seat** (*First Years/Kiddie*) has high arms and back and fits all adult toilet seats except padded ones. Grip locks hold the seat securely in place. Soft deflector is removeable. Suggested retail price under $12.

The **Freedom Trainer** (*G.W. Dmka/Best Days*) stepladder adapter is attached to a seat that fits atop the toilet. It has handles for extra security and folds up for storage and comes with a convenient hanging hook. Suggested retail price under $20.

The **Training Ring** *(Michael Friedman Corp)* with the molded, attached deflector in yellow plastic has an outer square shape. Suggested retail price under $3.

The **I-HO Toilet Trainer Seat** *(Primex Co)* has a back hinge that adheres to the top of an adult toilet with a small strip of adhesive tape. It lifts up to be out of the way for use by other family members. Suggested retail price under $5.

The **Topper** *(Century)* adheres to the lid and also lifts up to not interfere with adult use. Suggested retail price under $15.

Inflate-A-Potty *(Brite-Times)* is a vinyl blow-up blue and white portable potty that is used with 8-gallon disposable kitchen bags. Suggested retail price under $15.

The **Folding Potty Seat** *(Children on the Go)*, available from Practical Parenting *(page 108)*, folds up to 6"x 7½". Unfolded, it sits on top of adult toilet seats. It has overhanging corners for extra stability and hinges that don't pinch. Suggested retail price under $10.

Footstools for Solid Footing

You should have a sturdy footstool available to help your child get up on the adult toilet adapter seat. This is also helpful for the child who has learned to use the adult toilet without an adapter seat. And a stool can be of value for a small boy who isn't tall enough to urinate over the edge of the toilet bowl. It also gives a child having a bowel movement a solid footing to push and bear down on. Footstools can be used afterward to reach the sink and wash hands—an important habit that needs to be established early. Quality wooden footstools are expensive but they are usually a good, long term investment as you will find many uses for them over the years in various parts of your home. Many multi-use potty chairs, as we have mentioned, turn into footstools. But any footstool will do. A good footstool is important to have—probably more so—than even a potty chair.

As far as toilet training my daughter, I've decided to leave it up to her (future) husband!

Lynn Souter, Onalaska, WI

I know lots of people have used stickers as rewards during toilet training. We let my son choose a sticker and put in on the inside of the lid of the toilet. It worked like a charm, and looks cute, too.

Susan Boozier, Irvine, CA

Direct Use of the Toilet

It is perfectly acceptable to have your child learn to use the toilet without any special equipment. Obviously, the longer you wait to train your child, the bigger he or she will be and the more likely able to sit on an adult seat without any aid except possibly yours.

Remember the adult toilet can seem like an abyss to a child. But certain techniques can make a child feel more secure.

- Teach a boy to urinate sitting down backward on the toilet, straddling it, and pointing his penis downward. If he is distracted while standing, he might forget to aim.

- Teach a little girl to sit sideways or backward on the big toilet. A little girl should also "sink" her bottom low enough so urine does not go through the seat ring and bowl rim. In the beginning, removing underwear and pants will lessen chance of them getting wet.

- Hold your child securely on the seat's edge yourself.

T.P. Control

Learning moderation in the use of toilet paper is part of the training process.

- Impress upon a child that four squares of toilet paper will do the job effectively! Another measuring trick is to roll the paper down until it touches the floor. Or have a child take a strip of tissue the length of his or her arm.

- Reduce the use of excessive paper by making it harder to unroll. Before putting a roll of paper in place, press against it with the palm of your hand, in effect, squishing its natural contour. Now it will not turn as readily, increasing the chance of a child only taking what is needed, not what is easily unrolled.

- For a child who treats T.P. as an object of play, keep it off its natural holder for now but within reach. Place a rubberband around the roll that will be easy for you to remove but will be an obstacle for your child.

25

- Or cut off a center section the same size as the horizontal dimension of a roll of toilet paper from an empty plastic liter pop bottle. With a slit up the side (and trimmed to fit) it will act as a see-through cover to the toilet paper roll that will be easy for you to slip on and off the roll but virtually impossible for a child's small hands. (*Also a good deterrent for pets who think T.P. is for playing!*)

- Put the roll on *backward* so the paper comes from the back. Usually a child "slaps" paper down—not up—so there's less chance of excess unrolling.

Hygiene

Wiping seems to remain a parental responsibility for quite a while, even after a child has assumed much or all of the other responsibilities associated with toilet training, mainly because it is difficult for children to do a good job. Poor cleanup can be irritating, in more ways than one.

Stressing Good Habits from the Beginning

- Teach a child, especially a girl, to wipe from front to back. (Wiping from back to front can cause infections.)

- Let your child use premoistened babywipes after bowel movements. They are easier to use and many parents claim their use cuts down dramatically on laundry.

- Help your child understand that he or she should keep using new pieces of paper until there is no brown stain.

- Insist that hands be washed after using the toilet, and supply pretty hand towels and liquid soap to make the task less boring.

- Attach a hand towel to a towel bar with a shower curtain clip. That keeps it accessible yet off the floor.

Chapter 3

How Do I Begin Toilet Training?

❦

Toilet training is a learning process, not a disciplinary process, and a complicated one at that! Your child has to understand what you want, and then has to learn how to do it. In addition to understanding the bodily sensations, getting to the bathroom and getting clothes off, a child must first constrict sphincter muscles to achieve control, and then relax them to eliminate. Obviously there is a lot to learn. Gaining bowel and bladder control is a skill and fortunately children usually like to learn new skills.

The mastery of skills usually follows a pattern. First comes *bowel regularity* often followed by *bowel control. Daytime bladder control* often comes next but for many children this can happen simultaneously, and finally later (often much later), comes *nighttime bladder control.*

Not every child will follow this pattern, of course. While girls often achieve control before boys, brothers have been known to be dry before same-age sisters. Also, it is not uncommon, especially for boys over the age of 3, to have bladder control but not have bowel control. And, of course, there are children who achieve daytime and nighttime control simultaneously. With the swing toward a more relaxed approach to toilet training from the previous generation, children tend to be trained later and more frequently their bowel and bladder functions come under their control at the same time.

If you do choose a passive, more laissez-faire attitude about toilet training, keep in mind that children still need to know what it is that is expected of them. You are not necessarily "pushing" your child by providing direction and expectations. Some children really are ready to be trained early, so you are not "pushing" if you are meeting no resistance. Let their resistance be your guide. Children really do love learning grown-up behavior, so don't deny them their opportunity, if it fits their readiness.

My son was potty trained in three days at the age of 18 months. I had a potty chair in our bathroom. The trick was he *always* mimicked his daddy. (Daddy did have to sit down for a while, though!)
Rose M. Arndt Kurturin, Knox, IN

Bowel Control

At some point your child will no longer have bowel movements during the night. They do become a daytime process for most children. The more regular your child is, the easier it will be to start bowel-control training. Children often stop playing when they are having a BM. Some even hide in a favorite spot. Others just grunt or get red in the face. Saying, *"I see you're having a BM"* helps a child identify what is occurring and associate those sensations with the process.

Constipation, as explained in greater detail on page 31, if part of your child's history, may actually delay toilet training for your child. This is not anything to be worried about, but just one more variable you can be sensitive to.

Explain to your child that you will be taking him or her to the toilet or the potty chair and that you expect the bowel movement to go there rather than in diapers. *"This is what Mommy and Daddy do, what grown-ups do and now what you should do because you're getting so big and grown up"* is the kind of language to use. Give advance notice about when this procedure will start. Children need to hear what you expect in pleasant tones and words. They can't read your mind. Your attitude, your anticipation, your relaxed tones will also convey much of the message.

- If your child has a regular time for a bowel movement, choose that time to go to the bathroom.

- If there is no regular time, try within 30 minutes after a meal. When the stomach is full, the colon is often stimulated to empty.

- Consider putting feces into the potty container to show the child where it goes, as some parents have.

- Be prepared to sit with your child to keep him or her company. Don't insist your child sit for more than a few minutes but only as long as he or she is comfortable.

- Know that some children need to be alone to have a bowel movement. Bright bathroom lights and too much conversation may inhibit them from relaxing their sphincter muscles.

- Praise your child for every bowel movement made in the potty or toilet. Also praise a child for even sitting and trying to go.

- If your child will still be wearing disposable diapers at this point, you will be involved in getting them on and off. Keep masking tape on hand to refasten clean ones.

POWERS PUBLIC LIBRARY

To Flush or Not to Flush: That Is the Question

It is not unusual for a child to find such satisfaction in passing a bowel movement that he or she wants to keep or to play with the feces and will resist having them flushed down the toilet. You may need to leave them in the toilet a few minutes before flushing or do the flushing yourself after your child has left the bathroom, especially in beginning toilet training. Other children prefer to wave "bye-bye" and do their own flushing. Having control over the flushing can make it less scary for a fearful child.

While the child who views feces as modeling clay must be corrected, it is best not to refer to them as *"dirty"* or *"yucky."* A child may find it hard to forgive you or may feel demoralized by such comments. It may hurt a child to hear that this part of the body is bad or dirty and is being flushed away for that reason. Children may feel these words apply to themselves rather than to what they've "made." Explain that feces are the *"extras"* that your body doesn't need.

Belated Bowel Control

It is not uncommon for boys to achieve bladder control before—sometimes long before—bowel control. Parents sometimes feel that a child with belated bowel control is unwilling, uncooperative, or just plain stubborn but that's rarely the case. Again, patience is called for.

A reluctant-relaxer may require different approaches until you find one that works. Consider breaking the task

POWERS PUBLIC LIBRARY

into small, slow steps. Encourage a child to sit on and use the potty (or toilet) with clothes and a disposable diaper on to begin with. After a child is comfortable with this procedure, progress to going with only a disposable diaper—sides ripped open. Then you can move from sitting with a disposable diaper across the seat to just using toilet paper across it. Other children may be able to relax and void (just remove feces quickly with little fuss) while in a warm bath before making the transition to the potty chair or toilet. Or insist, that even using a diaper, a child stay in the bathroom when having a BM and then empty diaper into the toilet and flush.

Constipation is most often a factor in belated bowel control. A child who cries, screams, or kicks when urged to use the potty may be doing so because of the discomfort or pain experienced due to constipation. In this case, it is not stubbornness, but fear (real or imagined), that is keeping the child from doing what you ask and holding back. Some even believe there can be an inherited tendency towards constipation.

Constipation is NOT diagnosed by *infrequency* of bowel movements, but by the *hardness* and *character* of the stool. Dry BMs that don't stick to the diaper can be a description of constipation. And what may be considered hard to pass by adult standards is not the same for children. Whatever makes passing stool difficult or painful for a child will inhibit a child from wishing to repeat the procedure thus compounding the problem. Avoid suppositories and enemas as they will be seen as an "assault" by the child. The first step in treating constipation—actual or suspected—is to change the child's diet.

- Decrease milk products (milk, cheese, ice cream, etc.). If a doctor recommends eliminating milk products for any length of time, a calcium supplement will probably be recommended.

31

- Decrease or eliminate apples, bananas, rice, and gelatin. These are binders. Opt for peaches, instead.

- Chocolate is a constipating food especially when consumed in quantity. Some medications, too.

- Increase whole-grain breads, cereals, muffins, and any other bran foods. Try adding bran to other foods. If your child will only eat bran cereal with milk, and you're trying to cut down on milk, dilute the milk with water first. Offer graham crackers rather than soda crackers. Roughage helps.

- Possibly decrease fluid intake (milk, juices, sodas) to increase a child's appetite for bulkier foods. However, remember that fluids are important if you are dealing with constipation and shouldn't be drastically reduced. Encourage your child to drink water.

- Try prunes—the old standby—and dried fruits (if you can get your child to eat them!). Prune juice can be mixed with a small amount of milk. Encourage your child to eat fruits and vegetables with skins on, seeds, and berries for the fiber value. Fruit nectars are good too.

- Expect to wait two weeks or so before seeing a noticeable change in bowel movements after starting a new diet. Don't resume bowel training until such a change occurs.

Very *loose* stools can also inhibit bowel control but are often a sign of other problems (infection, milk allergy, etc.) indicating that a physician should be consulted. Food allergies causing chronic diarrhea can also cause "wear and tear" making it difficult to have bowel movements. A diet change may be recommended, but it should be done in conjunction with medical advice. But first just try eliminating apple juice—and other sweet juices—especially if your child drinks a lot, to see if that helps firm them up.

> When I was training my daughter, she would do *all* her business in her training pants until we decided she had to rinse out her own panties.
>
> *Rowena Cook, Anniston, AL*
>
> My son learned to urinate in the toilet when he was 2 years 7 months. However, he did not have the patience to sit and wait for a bowel movement. When he soiled his "big boy" pants, I asked him to remove his pants, pick up the stool with toilet paper, clean the floor and his underpants. After four days of this he decided it was lots easier to sit on the toilet!
>
> *Esta Drucker Sobey, Wilbraham, MA*

VERY Belated Bowel Control

Encopresis is the term used for lack of control of bowel movements for anyone over the age of 4. It is *NOT* uncommon. In fact it is reported that 1%–2% of children over age 4 are known as "fecally incontinent." For unknown reasons it is more common for boys than girls. It has incorrectly been assumed that this is the result of emotional disorders (which are more often the result—*not the cause*—of it) or by lax toilet training. A child can also be born with poor muscle tone in the bowel or anal sphincter. It seems, however, the majority of cases are the result of chronic constipation as discussed before, though of course it can be complicated by other stresses in either toilet training or life situations. With chronic constipation, colon tissue can be stretched to the point that nerves fail to receive proper signals and the muscles no longer contract properly so that a child no longer feels the urge to go.

...ild may even have no awareness of when stool ...ut into the underwear. Watery stools can also seep ...rder stool, soiling pants without a child being ... of it until after the fact. Regardless of the basis of the problem, both parents and children need to know they are not alone here and no one is to blame for this problem.

Not all doctors are trained in successful therapy for this problem so look to find one that is, as this problem needs to be approached medically as well as psychologically. If your county medical association can't help you, seek out a children's hospital or university teaching hospital near you. Encopresis is treated by a gradual retraining of the bowel which includes dietary changes, supplements, and behavior modification. There is not an overnight cure for this condition.

One helpful workbook for parents and children dealing with encopresis is *Childhood Constipation and Soiling* published by Dr. Dan Kohen, Behavioral Services of Minneapolis Children's Medical Center (*612-863-6900*).

Daytime Bladder Control

Some parents prefer to begin toilet training in the winter or rainy months when it's hard to get out of the house, but I think it is easiest to begin toilet training in the summer if this fits your schedule. Summer clothes are light and can be removed quickly. And when accidents do occur, you'll have fewer layers of clothes to launder.

If possible, plan to devote at least three days in a row to begin bladder training and give your child your complete concentration. During those days you must be able to drop everything when a child has to go.

- Tell your child that you expect to be told if there is a need to go.

- Let your child be in charge of as much of the toilet training process as possible.

- Put a child on the toilet first thing in the morning, before naps, after naps, after meals, after being dry for two hours, and before bedtime. Initially a regular schedule can help with this process.

- Keep your child company—unstrapped—on a potty chair or adapter. Use the time for reading. Books about potties are appropriate selections to keep in the bathroom!

- Praise all progress. For some, sitting more than 10 seconds may be progress.

- Turn the water on and let it run for "inspiration," or sprinkle warm water over a child's genitals.

- Offer more fluids when you are actively involved in training. The more a child drinks, the more a child will need to urinate and respond to body signals.

- Say occasionally *"it's time to try now."*

- Set a timer to remind your child when it's time to go potty rather than doing all the reminding yourself.

- Use the reminder as a "before" condition: *"After you use the potty, we will . . ."*

- Consolidate success by maintaining the same routine for several weeks.

Keep in mind that even children who have mastered the bathroom procedure may wet their pants during the day for several weeks or months.

If you have followed all reasonable steps for some time without success, stop! Try again in a few weeks or months.

For Boys Only

Aiming takes practice. When a little boy starts urinating in a standing position, be prepared to wipe up (and/or have him wipe up) around the toilet.

- Show a boy how to point his penis down to avoid spraying the room whether sitting down or standing up. (If a little girl wants to urinate standing up, explain why it doesn't work but let her try anyway if she wants to.)

- Teach your boy to aim accurately by having him *"sink the battleship."* Float the corner of an envelope or a piece of toilet paper in the toilet and have him aim at it. (Cherrios, we hear, are also popular for target practice!)

- Urinating into blue toilet bowl water will turn it green. (This works with girls too but it's harder to see.)

- In the summertime, and in the privacy of a backyard or woods, let a boy practice his aim.

- Let fathers and sons have a *"peeing party."*

- In the winter let a boy *"write in the snow."*

- If a little boy wants to stand but needs to be a bit taller, stand behind him and let him stand on your feet.

- Be sure the toilet seat can't fall down on a young boy in these early stages. Have your child check to be sure that the seat is up securely before he urinates.

- Start teaching your son NOW that the toilet rim needs to be placed down after he's finished!

During my 18-month-old son's bedtime, he would pee while standing up. We gave him a plastic cup to pee into. He was able to feel in control watching what was happening and learning to stop and start. He's not ready for toilet training yet but I think we've got his attention and that's half the battle.

Teresa Fix, Carbondale, IL

My son's ability to aim had to be curtailed when he *aimed* over our balcony into the living room.

Name withheld on request

With a rubber glove and a red crayon, I drew a bull's eye in the bottom of our toilet. My two year old son was delighted. It made toilet training a *"hit"* rather than a *"miss"* operation.

Jolene Smith, Redlands, CA

Target Training

To motivate and encourage good aim, you can purchase *Tinkle Time Targets* (Little White House)—small
flushable, nonstaining targets with animals or pictures. When the target is *"hit,"* it sinks! Each package
contains 45 targets. Suggested retail price is under $5.
They are available in stores or by mail from The Right
Start Catalog *(800-548-8531)*, One Step Ahead *(800-
274-8440)*, or Hand in Hand *(800-872-9745)*.

Dress for Success

Some parents feel that disposables are a real hindrance to
toilet training. Those wonderful absorbing qualities of
disposables prevent a child from feeling wet. And since
children—like adults—don't enjoy this wet sensation, less
absorbent diapers or pants can become a good motivator.

Going shopping with your child to buy training or
"fancy" pants has often been one successful tactic. You'll
probably find your child's favorite current cartoon character gracing them. Pretty ones are also available by mail
from catalogs like Biobottoms *(800-766-1254)*.

Switch from diapers to pants when your child is urinating in the potty several times a day. Better yet, ask your
child if he or she wants to try training pants. Be flexible,
though, and go back to diapers if they're more convenient
for you or if the child wishes to. Some parents like to make
the switch in stages, putting pants on a child for a few
hours in the morning and gradually extending the time.

- For one attention-getting way to start toilet training,
  keep your child pantless or, if this makes you uncom-

fortable, in loose-fitting underpants (nylon panties for girls) with elasticized waistbands. Without diapers, many children are more motivated to go to the toilet on their own. Plastic pants may retard "leakage" but they do make a wet diaper feel more comfortable—quite the opposite of the effect you want. The feel of lightweight pants often help children associate the idea of elimination with the need to control it. Sensations of wet and cold are immediately obvious which is not always the case with diapers and training pants.

- Be sure clothing is easy to pull off and on. Avoid buttons, zippers, snaps, and belts during this period.

- Consider attaching Velcro tabs to overalls to make them easy for a child to undo.

- Buy a sample cotton training pant larger than your child's present size—they often shrink—and wash them before a child wears them. If they are too tight around the legs, they will be difficult to raise and lower. Once you know which ones you and your child like, buy as many as your budget realistically allows.

- If pull-on pants are too hard for your child to manage, try using a diaper wrap with Velcro closings. Diaper wraps are absorbent, machine-washable diaper covers often including a waterproof outer layer.

- Change diapers (cloth or disposables) more frequently so a child gets use to and prefers the sensation of a dry, clean diaper.

- Take advantage of Huggies Pull-Ups Disposable Training Pants, with side stretch panels that allow children to slip them on and off like underwear. Tear-away sides allow for easy removal if needed. They come in three sizes: *small* fits children 19–28 pounds; *medium* fits children 29–38 pounds and *large* is for children over 39 pounds and up to 59 pounds. (A competitive brand, Drypers Big Boy-Big Girl Training Pants, comes in *medium* and *large* sizes.) Keep in mind, that like most disposables, these don't allow the parent or child to be aware of the feeling of wetness.

Cloth Options in Daytime Training Pants

Most of us turn to pull-up training pants for that transitional time when children need to experience easy-to-remove cloth underwear that also offers extra absorbancy. In addition to what your local store might carry, these are some options available to you:

Sara's Prints *"Try Hard" Training Pants* in sizes 2, 3, 4 come in double layered combed cotton in a variety of pretty patterns—separate ones for boys and girls. Suggested retail price under $8 each. By mail from Biobottoms *(800-766-1254)*.

Nikky *Pull-on Training Pants* in white have a waterproof layer sandwiched between 2 layers of cotton terry. Available in 4 sizes from 22 pounds up to 43 pounds. Suggested retail price under $12. Available from One Step Ahead *(800-274-8440)*, Baby Bunz & Co. *(800-676-4559)*, The Natural Baby Co. *(609-737-2895)*, and Baby Works *(800-422-2910)*.

Dappi *Early Trainer* is an absorbant pant with a nylon taffeta outer liner. Available in 3 sizes that fits 25 pounds to 35 plus pounds. Suggested retail price under $7. By mail from TL Care *(415-626-3127)*.

Nighttime Control

When we expect children to stay dry at night we are asking them to maintain a newly learned mastery of involuntary muscles—while they are asleep! This is no easy task. It's best not to make a big deal about nighttime control for a recently daytime-trained child. If you do, the child's anxiety about the problem could delay nighttime dryness for months.

Continue using diapers at night, but praise a child who wakes up dry. Remember that failure to achieve nighttime control is not willful in young children. Developmental readiness for daytime control is not the same as developmental readiness for nighttime dryness.

It should come as no surprise that nighttime bladder control can follow daytime control by anywhere from several months to several years. Maturation is usually what brings it about. There is really very little a parent can do to help a child establish nighttime control, at least until school age is reached.

Be aware that the occasional bed-wetting of preschool and early school years, and even a later return to bed-wetting, are not the same as persistent enuresis. (See page 89 for further discussion.)

My 2-year-old daughter just couldn't seem to make it through the night consistently without wetting, so we're back to diapers at night only. She was so relieved when I suggested it that I felt foolish for waiting so long. She'll grow to readiness, and in the meantime, it's no big deal!
Penny Dunmire, Avonmore, PA

Helping Your Child, Practically Speaking

- Restrict fluid intake, especially before bedtime. If you haven't ended night bottles, now is probably the time to do so. Kids just drink less from cups! Don't give sweet juices or sodas (especially colas and orange soda, because they contain caffeine), but don't deny a thirsty child a drink of water. Some say that going to bed thirsty just fixes a child's mind on water and increases the chances of nighttime wetting.

- Encourage your child to drink more during the daytime as kids often don't drink enough during the day if they are in daycare and try to make up for it in the evenings.

- Have your child use the toilet just before climbing into bed. Encourage complete voiding of the bladder or have the child go back to the toilet a second time. Or encourage a child to go twice by directing him or her to void at the beginning of the bedtime process and again, just before lights out. Encouraging a child to "push" it all out also helps exercise the muscle that helps hold it all in.

- Make sure the way to the bathroom is lit, even if only with night-lights. Draw a map with your child showing the way from the bed to the bathroom to help form a visual image.

- Invest in an automatic sensor light in the bathroom that comes on automatically when someone enters the room.

- Keep the house warm enough so the child won't avoid getting up because it's too cold. You can return to energy savings later.

- Consider keeping a potty chair near your child's bed if that will make things easier.

- Practice "positive imaging" as you put your child to sleep. Help a child imagine staying dry all night and waking up dry in the morning. Talk about the pleasure of feeling dry, in control, and grown-up.

- Whisper "dry" ideas into the ear of a sleeping child. (Some psychologists say children are often receptive to such "idea planting" during certain periods of sleep.)

- Let your child know that you know that he or she will stay dry at night "soon," like other big kids. It is important to set up the expectation, but don't subject your child to heavy pressure.

- Remove diapers and replace them with training pants, cloth soakers, or disposable Pull-Ups only after a week or so of dry nights.

While I was toilet training my daughter, I went into her room several times while she was asleep and gently whispered in her ear, asking her not to wet her bed. To my surprise, she awoke totally dry and eagerly ready to use her potty. For the next two days, I gave her chocolate as a reward for using the potty and continued my nightly suggestions while she slept. Gradually I stopped giving her the chocolate every time, but continued praising her for a job well done. Suddenly, she was trained (both bladder and bowel, day and night) in less than a week. But when I stopped the nighttime suggestions, she started wetting the bed again. I went back to making the suggestions, and gradually tapered off. Some may dispute the validity of this method, but for me, it worked like a charm!

Sherry Weinstein, Scotch Plains, NJ

Keeping Bedding Dry

- Wake your child to urinate before you retire. Doing this doesn't necessarily train a child, but it keeps the bed dry for some and leads to nighttime control for others. If your child is almost impossible to wake up, or becomes angry when awakened, don't try this method if under 5 years of age.

- Keep your child in diapers for sleeping. Double diaper pads may be necessary, or you can line the inside of a diaper or pant with a sanitary napkin for extra absorption.

- Putting a plastic or rubber pant over a toddler-sized disposable diaper prevents leakage for some.

- Keep a flannelized rubber sheet, a plastic tablecloth, or a shower curtain between the sheet and the mattress before, during, and for some time after nighttime training. Wetproof Snug 'n Dry flannel bed and crib sheets made by Americare (*800-220-CARE*) are in many stores.

- Wrap a large terry-cloth beach towel midway around the bed over a moisture barrier as mentioned above, tuck it in at the sides, and remove it if it gets wet during the night.

- Keep a sleeping bag on hand for a child to finish off a night's sleep if you are not up to changing wet sheets in the middle of the night.

- See additional ideas on pages 98–103.

> **Tell a child who wakes in the night to go to the toilet whether or not he feels the need to go. Children sometimes wake up and don't know why. Impress upon your child that his body woke him up for a reason and it was probably to use the toilet.**
> *Rena Manthei, Houston, TX*

Cloth Pants For Nighttime Use

If you have a preference for cloth, and many do, there are several brands and styles available to you. What you don't find in a store, you can find by mail today!

Nikky *Super Absorbent Bedwetter Pants* with extra protection with a water-proof barrier that is sandwiched between cloth layers. For ages 3, 4, 5 as well as for 6–7, 8–9 and up to 15. Suggested retail $19–$26. Available from One Step Ahead *(800-274-8440)* and Baby Works *(800-422-2910)*.

Stay Dry Pants are pull-on cotton pants, with a waterproof knit outer shell, that absorb up to a cup of urine for kids 18 pounds to 60 pounds. Suggested retail price under $25. Available from Biobottoms *(800-766-1254)*.

(See pages 96–97 for options of large nighttime disposables.)

Chapter 4

What Do the Experts Say?

One thing the experts (it's the *professional* experts we're talking about here) agree on is that you can't toilet train a child until he or she is ready—physically as well as emotionally. Another is that the age of readiness varies widely from child to child.

Most experts, including Benjamin Spock, M.D., T. Berry Brazelton, M.D., and Penelope Leach, Ph.D., recommend waiting for the child to show signs of readiness (usually at 2 or later), and using suggestions instead of pressure during the training process. They all advocate rewarding success with flattery and praise.

In *Dr. Spock's Baby and Child Care* (Pocket Books), Dr. Spock's advice reflects the conventional wisdom. His recommendation is to use a potty chair for a child up to age 2½ rather than a toilet seat adapter (but to use a foot stool here if you do), but he admits that it's not a matter of critical importance. He recommends letting a child become friendly with the potty chair before introducing the idea of using it for BMs and urinating. He also adheres to the idea that the potty should not be emptied by the adult until after the child has left the room or the toilet flushed until the child loses interest in the stool before flushing, believing that for a child under 2½ it is probably too frightening. Let children play bottomless once a child has expressed a real interest but if accidents occur return to diapers. He indicates that belated back sliding on bowel control is more of a control issue causing constipation rather than the current theories that constipation is often the culprit. Spock suggests leaving nighttime training to the natural maturing of the bladder.

Dr. Brazelton's method follows a simple format. First, have your child sit (fully dressed) on a potty chair at least once a day. After that ritual is accepted, undress your child and take him or her to the potty chair. Aim for a time when your child is likely to have a bowel movement. Praise successes, but don't overdo it. If you feel your child is ready, have your child play with no clothes on from the waist down, and make it clear that it is the child's responsibility to go to the potty chair when necessary. If your child loses interest and doesn't cooperate, go back to diapers and try again in a few weeks.

Penelope Leach, Ph.D., in *Your Growing Child* (Knopf) talks about the delicate balance to be struck in toilet training between parents' need to be clear about their preference for a child to use the potty or toilet but to avoid the temptation to use toileting as a battleground. Once a child is aware of the "feeling-product" connection, a child should be told that urine and feces should be put in a potty or toilet like grown-ups do. She feels one should keep interference of a child's daily activities to a minimum. If you keep reminding a child to sit on the potty you can ruin the whole process. A potty seat's portability allows it to be brought to where the child is so a child can take responsibility yet not have to run to find a potty when muscle control can't excercise that kind of delay. Avoiding diapers is recommended and be prepared for puddles. Compliment with pleasure but don't go overboard with congratulations.

Louise Bates Ames of the Gessell Institute of Child Development sees each generation as calmer about this developmental task than its predecessor. She still recommends the use of the newspaper-on-the-bathroom-floor routine for a child (and usually a boy) who insists on squatting for a BM and refuses to use either a potty seat or the toilet until this stage passes.

A bestselling toilet training book that has made enthusiastic converts of some and sparked controversy among others is *Toilet Training in Less Than a Day* by Nathan Azrin, Ph.D., and Richard Foxx, Ph.D., (Pocket Books, 1974). The program these two psychologists recommend was first devised not for speed, but to help the retarded learn this difficult skill. Later, it was adapted for the average child. Some people feel that the program is overly manipulative and, in some aspects, actually punitive. Others object to the heavy use of sweet drinks, sweets, and salty treats.

The demands on both parent and child are considerable. One whole day must be devoted to training, with no distractions whatsoever. The authors recommend that trainer and trainee be confined to the kitchen, where cleanup is comparatively easy. Here's a brief summary of the procedure:

1. The parent provides a doll that wets and, with prompting from the parent, the child "trains" the doll in the prescribed manner.

2. Liquids are offered constantly, on the theory that the more urine that is produced, the more quickly the training will be accomplished. Salty snacks are given freely, if necessary, to increase appetite for the liquids.

3. The parent is given a sequence of reminders to use, ranging from a firm "go now" to questions about the need to go and general suggestions.

4. The child goes to the potty, pulls down his or her pants (very loose ones are recommended), and sits there for ten minutes, or until urination occurs. The child wipes himself or herself and pulls up the pants.

5. Four rewards are given for every success: verbal praise, nonverbal reinforcement (hugs and kisses), something good to eat, and references to "friends who care" (*"Grandma will be so pleased"; "Tommy goes in the potty, too"*).

6. Disapproval is expressed when there's an accident, although ". . . spanking or other physical punishment is probably never justified." The child is then required to practice hurrying to the potty from different places in the house 10 times (*yes, 10!*), to feel the pants in order to tell the difference between wet and dry, and finally, to do all the necessary cleanup.

Does it work? Many say it does. And in a formal study of children 20 months to 4+ years of age, Azrin and Foxx found that success was achieved in periods ranging from a half hour to two days, with the average being about four hours.

Responses to a question about the method in my *Practical Parenting*™ *Newsletter* (*no longer in-print*) varied:

"Toilet Training in Less Than a Day was our biggest help. (My son was 2 years, 9 months.) The two disadvantages were 1) it was very boring for me, and 2) you really should stay home for a week to be sure the method has stuck. Very much worth it."

Nancy Holte, Cannon Falls, MN

"Unless your child is eager to please you in general, the boundaries [in this book] are so rigid that you may have a major battle on your hands."

Elaine Whitlock, Northhampton, MA

"I have come to the conclusion that when your child is ready, he'll do it. I used *TTLD* for my first son when he was about 3 years old, and it worked! It was wonderful, and I told everyone about that book—until I tried with son No. 2, and it failed miserably! Now, seven months later, he's trained, and to this day I still don't know what caused it to happen other than that he was ready, that all the explaining, practicing—not to mention the big-boy pants with the trucks on them—finally clicked, and he understood."

Nance Don, Washington Township, NJ

Using Rewards

Toilet Training in Less Than a Day emphasizes the reward system, which has raised a major concern for parents. Many parents feel strongly that any kind of material reward is wrong or simply inappropriate when a child is learning basic proper behavior. Others don't object at all. And some object only to the use of sweets. The biggest concern of those offering rewards are, "*How and when do I stop?*" "*Will my child expect a treat or gift every time he or she visits the bathroom for weeks, month . . . years?*"

According to parents who have used the reward system, this is not a problem. It is easy to run out of whatever you are using after a few weeks. The kids do accept that. And a reward system can be an effective motivator!

You can differentiate rewards as you progress. When your child either asks to go without prompting (and makes it to the potty on time) or spontaneously uses the potty independently or attains a certain number of dry days, might be the time for a "larger" reward that has been previously discussed.

Use your imagination for rewards (you know your

child best), and consider combining material rewards with nonmaterial ones. For some children, the most effective reward might be calling Grandpa or Grandma to report a "success" (*this obviously works best if grandparents live within local dialing distance!*); for others, it's stickers or stars on a chart or calendar. One child I know was motivated by the promise of wearing a swimsuit all day long if there were no accidents, while a set number of pushes on a swing did the trick for another child.

Placement of any tangible rewards to be handed out is helpful too. They should be in sight but out of reach. A large, clear cannister or bowl is one way to accomplish this. Or maybe having an assortment of small wrapped items stored in the bathroom.

Rewards can be a helpful incentive but they *WON'T* toilet train a child who is not *READY* to be trained. If, after a few days or week, training is not working, forget it—rewards as well as your efforts! Back off. For some children, their egos get too wrapped up with the prize and they (as well as parents) miss the point of this exercise!

The best reward is often not a material reward at all. It is self reward! In addition to praise and pleasure expressed by adults, encourage self-praise. Teach your child to give him or herself a *"pat on the back."* Or suggest to your child *"Give yourself a hand"* so your child can self-applaud for a job well done. (*Of course, you can add to the applause too!*)

Our son would willingly pee in the toilet or potty but a bowel movement he would only do in his pants. My husband came up with the ideas of "pennies for poos"—which worked for us. It was better than sweets and boosted his bank balance. We now have a 6-month-old girl and we've already started saving change!

Mary Jackson, Staten Island, NY

Material Rewards to Consider

- M&M Plain Chocolate Candies.

- Jelly beans, chocolate kisses, or other favorite candies.

- Sugarless candy or gum.

- Raisins: one for using the toilet, another for wiping, another for flushing, another for washing hands, etc.

- Pieces of fruit, crackers, a special cookie, or what ever treat is your child's favorite.

- A box of animal crackers—to be eaten one at a time from a box which is easily visible.

- An ice cream cone.

- A penny for each *"success"*—two, perhaps, for a bowel movement.

- A new book.

- Big-boy pants or fancy big-girl pants (or a shopping trip to get them).

- A dollar for spending in the local variety store.

- A sugarless gumball from a toy gumball machine (not for children under 3 years of age).

- The promise of a really grand gift (a fish, a gerbil, special toy, a trip to the zoo) after a week or two of continuous success—and then provide it right away!

"It Worked for Me"

We used a *Potty Box* with candy for rewards. A funny side effect was that the other mothers who had been so disapproving of our *Potty Box* soon noticed that their kids never had accidents when visiting us!

Lisa Smith, Hurst, TX

My mother-in-law ordered me to give M&M's as rewards for correct potty performance. Unfortunately my son responded too well and I ($9\frac{1}{2}$ months pregnant at the time) was having to jump up every ten minutes to give him another chocolate and verify that he did the job. I switched to raisins, but he did not like them as much and went back to wetting his training pants. A few months later, he gradually became dry.

Lucy Tierney, Slidell, LA

I think giving candy or little gifts is very wrong. I tacked a calendar to the wall in the bathroom at his eye level. Every time he went potty, he got a star on that day. (I bought those colored stick-on stars.) Some days he only had two stars; other days half a dozen. It worked for us!

Linda Miner, Berkeley, CA

For rewards, we used up two boxes of Life Cereal and spent $15 on new books. I think it was cheaper than another few weeks of Pampers.

Susan Ringer, Florence, MS

Beyond Rewards

Sometimes we need that extra motivation that goes beyond buying a potty seat, verbal praise, and even rewards to remind children of what's expected.

Gentle inspiration can come in the form of books, videos, games, and even potty-training dolls. Some potty-training books may seem a bit silly to parents, but they're often adored by children because they relate to them so completely. The books demonstrate a developmental step with language and pictures a child can understand, and the characters provide role models. They clearly show what's expected of a child, which we sometimes forget to relay consistently.

Doing it by the Book

For parents, books are helpful because they take some of the work off our shoulders and provide a point of departure for a casual discussion on the subject with a child.

Share the books with any caretaker who might spend time with your child. This can be grandparents, babysitters, daycare providers, or older children who read to toddlers.

Don't be surprised if potty books become a source of fascination and love to be read and reread and reread. So be sure to buy one or more that you can listen to repeatedly.

I read *more* books while each of my three sat on the potty chair! The books were used as a distraction. It seemed to be useless to say, *"Here's the potty, now go!"*

Nedra O'Neill, Calumet Park, IL

Some available books that many parents have found helpful appear on the following pages.

KoKo Bear's New Potty
by Vicki Lansky
Bantam Books

This delightful, full-color, 32-page illustrated story of KoKo (a unisex bear) who learns to use the toilet, will please parent and child alike. (*Granted, we are biased.*) All the steps in this growing-up process are explained to the child, and each page also contains tips to guide the parent through the progress and setbacks that are normal encounters.

Once Upon a Potty—His
Once Upon a Potty—Hers
by Alona Frankel
Barron's

This is a small hardcover book with color illustrations that are great fun. It is the story of a small boy—Joshua (or girl—Prudence) who is introduced to a floor-model potty, has some problems with timing and placement, but ultimately learns to get the "wee-wee" and "poo-poo" in a pot-style potty. The story is a bit silly and may turn some parents off, but it seems to delight most children.

I Have to Go
A Sesame Street Toddler Book
Random House

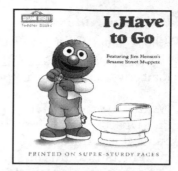

Little Grover runs past favorite characters on Sesame Street saying, "I have to go," until he finds his Mommy, who understands and drops everything to help Little Grover find his potty. The story ends with Little Grover and his Mommy very pleased and proud.

Going to the Potty
by Mr. Rogers
G. P. Putnam's Sons

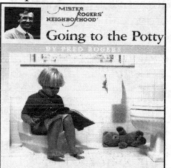

This 32–page photo book in full-color shows children of different ages, sexes, and ethnic backgrounds using the potty correctly and helps a child know what to expect. The short story line is told in the gentle fashion we have come to associate with Mr. Rogers.

Your New Potty
by Joanna Cole
Morrow Junior Books

In a charming, full-color photo essay, you will follow one girl and one boy's use of the potty, graduation to underpants, and ultimately the toilet. The lanugage used is "urine" and "BM" for body functions.

I'm A Big Kid Now
A Book About Toilet Training
by Joane Graham Brooks, M.D.
Kimberly-Clark, Neenah, WI

Written to promote Huggies Pull-Ups disposable training pants, this is still a well-done introduction to training. Its 56 pages covers a story for boys, a story for girls, and information for parents in an attractive full-color book. For information about how to order, call *800-544-1847*.

Potty Time
by Betty Reichmeier
Random House

This Learning Ladder, 10 page, washable vinyl soft book will survive well in the bathroom. The story is of a child of an indeterminate gender who shows a large toy teddy bear how the process works. Basic but nicely done.

No More Diapers
by J. G. Brooks, M.D.
Delacorte Press

This two-part book includes a short preface for parents. Each part presents an illustrated story, one for boys and one for girls. Both stories show the child starting with a potty chair, taking responsibility for emptying it into the toilet, and learning to like feeling dry.

Toilet Learning
by Alison Mack
Little Brown

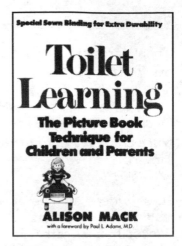

This durable paperback is divided into two parts. The first is a parent's guide to preparing yourself and your child for toilet learning. The second part is a colored-picture story that takes your child through the process of elimination, functions of bathroom "equipment," examples of all sorts of folks who use the bathroom, the way boys and girls differ in their use of the bathroom, and where we find bathrooms. The terms used for elimination are "wee-wee" and "doo-doo." However, parents are encouraged to substitute their own words.

Should this not be enough to satisfy your needs, here are a few additional titles you may come across or even wish to look for in a bookstore or library:

Annie's Potty by Judith Caseley *(Greenwillow)*
I Want My Potty by Tony Ross *(Kane/Miller)*
I Have to Go by Robert Munsch *(Annick Press)*
My Potty Chair by Ruth Young *(Viking Kestrel)*
On Your Potty by Virginia Miller *(Greenwillow)*
Potty Time by J. Langely and Anne Civardi *(Little Simon)*
Sam's Potty by Barbro Lindgren *(Morrow)*
The Potty Chronicles by Annie Reiner *(Magination Press)*
Toilet Tales by Andrea Wayne von Konigslow *(Annick Press)*

Should You Need More Inspiration . . .

If books are not your medium, maybe videos are. Here are two that are directed at children in an entertaining while enlightening format.

Once Upon A Potty for Him
Once Upon a Potty for Her
Barron's Home Video
800-645-3476

These videos are the animated and expanded versions of the book of the same name by Alona Frankel. It features a sing-along Potty Song and a pediatrician, at the end of the tape answering subject-related questions. 30 minutes. VHS.

It's Potty Time

Learning Through Entertainment
Video Distributors
Gastonia, NC 28052
800-445-5142

This video designed for children 2 and over, endorsed by Duke University Medical Center, uses songs and a story about a birthday party to teach the steps for toilet training and washing up. 25 minutes. VHS.

Surrogate Success Models

One very effective concept that many parents have used is letting their child toilet train a stuffed animal or doll. Many a Teddy has paved the way to successful use of the toilet. Dolls that wet and are ready for toilet training include *Baby Alive* from Kenner; *Betsy Wetsy, Tiny Tears, Magic Potty Baby* from Tyco Toys; and Hasbro has a *Cabbage Patch Kids' Potty Seat* for their dolls. But should you prefer to combine the doll straight from the pages of one popular toilet training story book for children, you can.

Once Upon a Potty Book and Doll
Barron's
800-645-3476

Packaged with the book and/or the video *(you need to specify "his" or "hers")*, you can purchase the soft doll and potty for your child to play with, train and model after.

And Games to Play

And if books and videos and dolls aren't enough, you can always make a game of it. And some have!

My Potty Game (Rock-A-Bye Baby, Inc., Pompano Beach, FL 33069, 800-762-5229) provides a large, colorful chart to attach stars (with Velcro) and a "crown" to encourage successes.

The Potty Game (Stopher Inc., Baltimore, MD 21209, 410-683-6987), developed by two mothers, includes a parents' manual, a *Dinosaurs Don't Wear Diapers* book, dinosaur stickers, and a sticker board. It provides children with an active role and positive reinforcements.

Chapter 5

Help! How Can I Toilet Train My Uncooperative Child?

❦

The standard line proffered to the mother of a child who's hard to train is, "No child has gotten on the school bus in a diaper yet." This, of course, is not much help if you are trying to figure out how to proceed.

If your child has progressed from the terrible twos to the formidable fours without showing the slightest interest in the toilet, your concern is justified. If your child prefers to squat, comfortably diapered, in a dark corner, holding a special blanket, you may be dealing with physical or emotional complications, irrational fears, or ingrained habit. You may have a willful child who needs some special handling, or you may be dealing with a simple problem in semantics.

It's also possible that your timing is off. Asynchrony is a big word that simply means that a child's "internal clock" is set differently from those of other members of the family.

Elimination may not occur when you think it should. For example, a child may have only one bowel movement in two days, or three in one day. If this is the case, it's you who will have to do the adjusting.

And, painful but true, you yourself may be causing the trouble. Ask yourself the questions listed in the box below. If you have two or three "yes" answers, perhaps you should sit back and do a little thinking. Try talking out your problems with your spouse, a friend, a doctor, or nurse practitioner—but *don't* take your frustrations out on your child.

Some Questions to Ask Yourself

- Are you determined to have your child toilet trained by a certain age or stage in his or her life, or at some special point in your own?

- Do you see your life as being in a shambles until your child is trained?

- Are you particularly sensitive to pressure from family or friends to "get that child to use the toilet"?

- Do you think your child is punishing you by not cooperating with your training efforts?

- Are you positive that because your child can understand you there's no reason toilet training can't be accomplished easily?

- Have you ever been described as a "controlling" parent?

- Are you strongly opposed to backing off for now and trying again in a month, when all the pieces might fall into place?

One possible solution might be to have someone else take over. Sometimes, for all our good intentions, we are simply too emotionally involved to get the job done. Some parents can't teach their own teenagers to drive, and wisely turn the task over to someone who's better able to deal with it unemotionally. This doesn't mean they're bad parents. In fact, they're to be congratulated for recognizing the problem and taking the proper steps to correct it. It's the same with toilet training. If you can see that the process is getting you too upset, and that you, in turn, are upsetting your child, try to find someone else with some emotional distance who can do it for you. And don't feel guilty! Part of being a good parent is knowing what you can and can't do. You won't prove anything by trying to do the impossible.

Physical Complications

If you suspect that it's a physical problem, have your child checked thoroughly by a physician.

- Consider the possibility of an allergy. Lactose intolerance (the inability to digest milk or milk products) is the most common, but other foods can cause allergies, too.

- How much sorbitol is your child consuming in sugarless candies and gum? Sorbital is a new culprit in chronic loose stools. It also is found naturally in pear juice and apple juice which could make a difference if a child drinks lots.

- Watch for signs of urinary infections. These include pain or burning sensations while urinating, straining to urinate, color changes in the urine, foul-smelling urine, frequent urination that produces very little, or a split stream of urine. Other signs could be abdominal pain or a fever of an undetermined origin. Such infections are not uncommon in small children.

- Be aware that even after a urinary problem has cleared up, the child may still remember and fear the pain of urinating, and this may complicate potty training. Reassure the child and don't be impatient if it takes him or her a while to get over the fear.

> My daughter at age 4 would often have accidents—to my distress. I thought she was being lazy and refusing to stop her play to take the time to go to the bathroom which she knew how to do. I was on her case a lot. At our annual physical, we discovered it was a physical problem. My guilt load was heavy for a long time.
>
> *Martha Berk, Louisville, KY*

- Check a toilet trained child who starts to have many urinary accidents, as well as a significant increase in urination for diabetes.

- Remember that diarrhea—persistent runny, loose stools can cause problems with bowel control. Persistent diarrhea is usually a symptom of a physical problem, and it should be treated by a doctor.

- Consider the possibility that constipation (see page 31) is keeping your child from wanting to move his or her bowels, because it is painful. If it's not chronic, you can help by keeping the children company while they're sitting on the toilet, lubricating the anus with Vaseline, or even helping hold the "cheeks" apart to make it easier to move the bowels. Dietary changes can also help. Chronic constipation can put pressure on the bladder and cause daytime, as well as nighttime, accidents in which case it's time to seek medical attention.

Emotional Complications

Don't hesitate to seek professional help if you think there's an emotional problem you can't solve. Getting help from a therapist doesn't mean that your child is in serious trouble, and you may find that things improve rapidly after only a session or two. Children are often more open with a neutral third party person than with a parent. Remember that children often keep silent about fear or shame they're feeling. Therapists are trained to help children learn to express and deal with these feelings.

- Remember that the emotional makeup of a human being is extremely complex. It's not realistic to expect that just because a child is small in stature, he or she will have a small range of emotions. And handling all these strange feelings and sensations is doubly hard for a child because of his or her undeveloped wisdom and lack of information.

- Watch for interference from others. Siblings can set a child off by playing on fears and expectations; friends or even teachers may say the wrong thing.

- Ask your child to show you how he or she would toilet train a doll or stuffed animal. Watch the child's behavior and listen carefully to commands and instructions. If the child uses abusive language, scolds, and handles the toy roughly, it might be a clue that your own or someone else's attitudes and actions are at fault.

- Or get the child to draw a picture of a bathroom. Ask for explanations of anything you don't understand. You may get some clues about worries or fears the child has been repressing.

Toilet Fears

Some children—especially those with older, storytelling siblings—believe the toilet is a hiding place for sharks, alligators, or water monsters. The sound of a toilet flushing may serve to confirm this. One mother on discovering that her child feared the monsters in the toilet, led her child to the bathroom, called the monsters up out of the toilet, and blew them out the window, much to the child's relief.

Don't flush the toilet while the child is still sitting on it. Many children find the noise and action frightening and worry about being "swallowed up." Showing a child how things work inside the toilet tank and taking the child to the basement to explain the workings of the plumbing system may banish this fear.

Willfulness

If you have a truly willful child, you will have seen stubbornness and other signs before now. They don't usually begin to appear just at this time. If you have seen the signs before, look back and remember how you've handled your stubborn child who sometimes digs in his or her heels and refuses to cooperate.

Sometimes a 3- or 4-year-old child stubbornly refuses to make a bowel movement in the toilet or potty and insists on diapers even when the child uses the potty or toilet appropriately when urinating. Sometimes a child even insists on taking underwear off and putting a diaper on just before a BM. It's frustrating because it's obvious the child feels the sensation of the coming BM and can exercise control to go when he or she wants to. In addition, children who retain BMs for any great length of time are more likely to become constipated. Sitting a child on the toilet for long periods is not necessary when a child understands how to use the toilet. Children who have been lectured or reminded too often, and forced to sit on the toilet for long periods of time against their will, may understandably be resistant to your pressure when control is the issue.

There is no single solution to this situation. For a child who might be stuck in this behavior and for whom even rewards don't work, and you don't think constipation (as described on page 31) is the problem, change your approach. Back off for a few weeks. Wait for a stress-free week, and then tell your child that when this box of diapers is gone you're not having any more diapers. Transfer all responsibility to your child explaining that *"It's your job to make your BM and get it into the toilet. You no longer need my help."* Explain also that it's okay if your child has a BM or wets but he or she can't walk around in soiled underwear. Clean clothes must be worn before engaging in any other activity. You can also :

- Consider using reverse psychology: *"Oh, I'm sure you won't want to use the potty today: we'll just put the diaper on."* Or switch roles: *"I need to go potty. Will you keep me company?"*

- Avoid "no" answers as much as possible by telling your child *"It's time to try"* instead of asking *"Do you have to go?"*

- Give choices: *"Do you want to help get your pants off and wipe yourself, or should I do it?" "Do you want to use the potty chair today or the big toilet?"*

- Physically lead the child to the toilet with a hand on a shoulder or arm, not roughly, but firmly enough so the child knows you mean business.

- Increase unconstipating foods (see page 32) at mealtime. Keep a matter-of-fact attitude in the face of tantrums and accidents, and show no annoyance.

- Think of your child just as a "late bloomer" to help you avoid feeling frustrated.

- Discuss this with your child's day-care provider as it may provide additional insights and offer you both new ways to handle this problem.

At age 3 my son refuses to have BMs on the potty. He insists on a diaper. I've pinpointed the problem— he just can't "perform" sitting down! On one hand, he becomes very upset if he does go in his pants, but if I suggest he sit on the potty, he insists he "can't." He had no trouble learning to urinate.

Sandra Heath, Brownsville, TX

- Completely back off. Possibly your style and your child's temperament are working against each other.

- Refer also to pages 30–31 for additional ideas.

Comprehension

Intelligent as your child may be, he or she may be missing a piece of the very complicated puzzle you're presenting.

- Examine the words and phrases you're using and ask yourself if your child could be interpreting any of them to mean something other than what you intend.

- Be at eye level with your child while you talk. Use the child's name and have him or her look at you to be sure you have his or her undivided attention.

- Test the child's comprehension by rephrasing your requests and instructions in the simplest language possible.

Chapter 6

How Can I Toilet Train a Child Under Special Circumstances?

❦

Sometimes toilet training must be attempted under conditions that are less than ideal, regardless of our preferences.

You start training a month before the new baby is expected, and then the baby comes three weeks early! Or training is progressing slowly, and you're only halfway there, three days before the family leaves for a long vacation.

You didn't opt for twins, but twins you have—and both are ready and eager to be trained at the same time. Maybe your day-care center started training procedures just before you are about to leave for a vacation. Or jury duty calls!

The greatest challenge is probably the one presented to parents of a child who is physically or developmentally handicapped or one who will ultimately be diagnosed as dyslexic. Severe problems such as these will require the advice and cooperation of your physician. Your physician will be able to give you information, resources and suggest reading material that will be helpful. Drs. Azrin and Foxx, the authors of *Toilet Training in Less Than a Day* have worked with those who have disabilities of one kind or another and have also written *Toilet Training for the Retarded* (Research Press, 1973).

The New-Baby Syndrome

If you have a choice, you probably won't want to start training a child just before or after the birth of a new baby. Before the birth, you won't be up to the running, and after the birth, you'll probably be too busy. So start several months before or several months after the fact. Remember your older child is going to see how much attention your new baby will be getting in activities like diapering and sometimes an older child just likes to regress to babyhood for desired attention. Wait until the baby is old news. But if you must go ahead with it, think about these things.

- Plan to give the child a great deal of attention. Take no shortcuts. Spend a lot of time alone with the child and do everything you can to set comfort and self-assurance levels as high as possible. *(Easy to say, I know.)*

- Involve your spouse or someone else in the process so your attention alone is not the sole motivating factor!

- Emphasize the grown-up aspects of being toilet trained, and choose whatever status symbols ("grown-up pants," treats) or other rewards you wish.

- If after two weeks you see few signs of success, postpone toilet training until you're sure your child is ready for it. Do not make the child feel guilty for "failing." (See *Regression*, page 86.)

Leah, almost 2, couldn't have chosen a worse time. I was nearly due with my third child and I knew siblings sometimes regress when a baby is born. I thought she should wait but she disagreed! I explained my theory of privilege and responsibility. *"If you want your diaper off, you must use the potty."* (To this day I'd rather deal with a messy diaper than messy pants.) She had to convince me—and she did. Her one accident seemed tragic to her and was never repeated.

Lois Slusky, Ferndale, MI

Working Parents

With most young mothers returning to work within 3 to 12 months after having a baby, toilet training today is often done by, or in conjunction with a childcare provider. Obviously, every caretaker (be it an in-house sitter, a home day care provider, or someone at a day-care center) will have her (or his) own style. Since there is no one magic way to train a child, working parents will need to integrate their system with the one a child is exposed to during the day.

If you are comfortable with the general discipline, style, and attitude of the environment your child is exposed to, the odds are you will also be comfortable with the system or process used for toilet training. Toilet training philosophies and techniques should be part of the interview process, expecially if you are interviewing a childcare provider when your child is 12 to 18 months of age.

Nursery schools (versus a day-care center) for children 3 and up usually require children to be toilet trained because of licensing requirements.

Day-care Dynamics

Group day care will provide a different dynamic from training one-on-one at home, but the principles are basically the same. One advantage of group day-care is that peer pressure often speeds up the process.

• Start good two-way communications before the process begins. Parents may want to begin training, but it is often the caregiver who may first see the signs of readiness. Tell your child's caregivers *before* you start toilet training, and ask them to do likewise. Some centers use the process of checking a child every half hour or watching for consistently dry periods of time every day, to use as an indication of readiness.

• Consider introducing toilet training for two weekends before the day-care provider begins. If it can be arranged, you might take some vacation days to at least get the process started at home.

• Using the same language and having the same attitude toward toilet training makes the adjustment from one environment to the other smoother and less confusing for your child. Also, if a reward system is used, make sure it's consistent between home and day-care.

• To keep the issue a priority, make sure you and your provider are in the habit of reminding your child about the various aspects of toilet training using similar language in questions such as, *"Are you dry now?"* or *"Do you have to go to the potty?"*

• Bring at least five changes of clothes and underwear to your child's day-care site every day during this process. Your child WILL have accidents and shouldn't be reduced to wearing a diaper by the end of the day.

- Check which kind of potty chair is used at your child's center as it might influence your method of training at home. Many centers, however, have very low, flushable child-sized toilets. (Also, find out if they use foot stools at the center.)

- Try to increase your fun time together after work before getting down to the business of toilet training if your quality time together is limited.

- Remember to dress your child in easy access clothes. It's probably not a good time to use overalls.

- Show an interest in your child's experiences using the potty at day-care by talking about them together.

- Be prepared to back off if your child does not show progress within 2 to 4 weeks or any agreed upon arrangement with your childcare provider. Sometimes they're just not ready regardless of preceived readiness.

- Be aware that some children who use the toilet appropriately at the center may not bother to do so at home. This is not an uncommon, though usually temporary, occurance.

Traveling During Training

Travel may or may not interfere with training. On a short trip, it probably won't; on a longer one, it may. Don't make your trip a battleground. You can work on toilet training when you get home.

Some children love the idea of a strange toilet, while others will absolutely refuse to use one. And, most frustrating, the same child may demonstrate both attitudes within a couple of months.

- If you anticipate extensive travel, consider opting for the adult toilet seat for toilet training rather than a potty chair. It will simplify your packing.

- Look into the purchase of travel-style adapters that fit into your bag such as the folding-style seat adapter featured on page 23.

> I explained to my daughter that the diaper I put on her was to be used only as a last resort, that she should tell me when she had to go, and we would try to find a restroom. This did not set back her toilet training at all. In fact, the few times when she did have to use the diaper, she was upset that she couldn't use a "big-girl potty." This phase lasted only a few months until she learned to control her bladder.
>
> *Cheryl Shephard, Brecksville, OH*

- Try to know the location of an acceptable rest room before you need it. For instance, when entering a museum check out the floor plan for restroom locations. With last minute announcements, little ones can't wait very long.

- Condition your child to the idea of using a variety of toilets in strange places by doing just that before your trip. Take the child into gas-station and department store restrooms; visit bathrooms in friends' homes and in restaurants. If you will be vacationing out-of-doors, practice those *"au natural"* methods.

- Take advantage of larger handicap booths when available to you so there is more room for you and your child.

- Explain how the bathroom on a train or airplane will look and sound.

- Pack a waterproof sheet or felt-back plastic tablecloth to go under the sheet to protect mattresses from an accident or leaking diapers. Even large plastic garbage bags will do.

- Pack some disposable diapers just in case your best-laid plans go awry. Trips are more important than momentary setbacks in toilet training.

> **Our 2-year-old was going through potty training while her older siblings were being driven to scouts, baseball practice, etc. She was afraid of the regular toilet so I'd bring her potty chair in the car with a small plastic garbage bag to line the potty chamber** *(plus toilet paper)* **and she'd always use her portable "out house." Afterwards I'd lift out the bag, tie and dispose of it. We never had wet pants!**
>
> *Linda Mahoney, Broomfield, CO*

Car Conveniences

No matter what you use enroute, do stop the car and pull over to the side when you child has to go.

- Carry a wide-mouth bottle, a large disposable, lidded soft drink cup, a coffee can or plastic ice-cream pail with a lid (that can also be used for motion sickness) for a child to urinate in. Any of these can also be used by a girl, if she sits tightly on the rim.

- Consider filling any of these containers halfway with the absorbant stuffing from a disposable diaper. It avoids "sloshing." If fact, for a boy urinating, all you need is a large resealable plastic bag stuffed with a disposable diaper.

POWERS PUBLIC LIBRARY

- Carry a potty chair or portable camping potty with you on a car trip.

Au Natural

Boys have the advantage out-of-doors when going behind a bush or the like. A girl needs help squatting and keeping her pants out of the way. If privacy permits, remove pants altogether. If squatting is problematic, crouch behind her, holding her out with your hands holding her bent knees and your elbows cradling her hips. Regardless, do carry diaper wipes for clean ups of hands as well as bottoms.

> As a pediatric nurse practitioner, I advise parents to accompany a child until they're around 7. Although mothers can take a boy into a ladies' room, fathers should not take a girl into a men's room, since unrinals are not private. A father should ask a woman to escort his daughter while he waits outside.
> *Meg Zweiback, R.N., P.N.P., Oakland, CA*

Using Public Restrooms Alone

The question of when to allow a child to use public toilet facilities unsupervised is a serious concern though parents seldom compare notes on this subject. Unfortunately this is a safety issue, and a real one at that. Once children 4 to 6 years of age prefer their own privacy and understand the differences between the mens' room and the ladies' room, you do need to respect their need for a same-sex facility, though most parents don't usually allow this to be a completely independent procedure until a child is over 7.

Women's rooms offer more privacy than those in men's

OWENS PUBLIC LIBRARY

rooms so it is more appropriate for children to come in with mom than it is to use the restroom with dad.

Always be prepared for facilities to be out of toilet paper. Carry purse-size tissue packages with you. Alert your child to check the toilet paper rolls first and to come to you ahead of time if none is available in any stall.

Despite the unkept appearance of some public restrooms, it is highly unlikely that any disease can be contracted from a toilet seat. Wiping a seat dry is adequate even when not aesthetically pleasing. Washing hands afterwards is, however, doubly important.

Supervised

- Stand outside the door while your child uses the facilities alone.

- Ask an appropriate-looking man to take a boy into the restroom while you wait outside the door. (*Same for situations with girls, Dad.*)

- Only let a child go alone to one that is in shouting distance or in view.

Unsupervised

Can your child perform all the neccessary tasks alone from locking the door to flushing to washing hands? Does your child have a healthy suspicion of strangers? If so, then it's time to let an interested child go alone. But still be alert to your child's whereabouts.

- Keep track of the amount of time your child is gone.

- Let two children go together.

   Some restrooms are never safe. Use your judgment and

let your children understand your standards and why. A child could use a familiar family-style restaurant restroom alone at a young age but should not be allowed to visit a bathroom in an out-of-the-way store facility.

This is a very difficult issue for me because of a rare, fatal case of abduction from a store's basement bathroom that occurred in our community. Francesca, age 5, insists on going to the bathroom alone. I stand outside, making sure there is only one entrance. I don't want to make my daughter nervous but she knows that if it's crowded or if anything she doesn't like happens to her, she's to *"come out and get mom,"* or just call out for me.

Nancy Tuminelly, Richfield, MN

Toilet Training Twins

Given the laundry or cost of disposables, there is the added economic incentive here to toilet train twins sooner. But their readiness, like singletons, is variable and usually later than our readiness. Some parents try to avoid training them at the same time, holding one off in any way possible, and others believe in plunging in and getting it all over at once.

Some people say that twins are not usually developmentally ready for toilet training until a little later than singletons are, but others disagree. There's such wide variation among children that the point has little validity anyway. When they're ready, they're ready.

Fraternal twins may vary as much in readiness as any other two children of the same age, with a boy likely to be ready somewhat later than a girl. Even identical twins may be ready weeks or months apart.

Sometimes problems arise with twins when one is both physically and emotionally ready for training and the other is not, but wants (or even demands) to share the experience. If you can manage to train them singly, even months apart, be grateful, and enjoy having just one in diapers.

- If you're training two at the same time, make things as easy as possible on yourself by moving gradually from diapers to training pants. Try pants for just a few hours a day, and when all of you are tired, change to diapers.

- Concentrate on treating the twins as individuals, not as a matched pair. Never compare the progress of one against the other. Don't impose one child's readiness on the other by comparing or blaming.

- Keep expressions of pleasure for the successes of one child low key enough so as not to set up competition for affection. And rewarding the successes of just one twin may cause the other to be resentful rather than to be motiviated. It will probably work best if both are rewarded for the successes of just one. There's a better chance both will be encouraged to try harder.

- Boys can share a toilet while urinating but with it will also come the tears and tantrums from the inevitable wetting of one by the other.

- Take advantage of the fact that a trained twin will be a perfect role model when the second is ready.

- Supply two potty chairs, in different colors, and assign one very specifically to each twin. It's not reasonable to expect that there won't be times when both have to use the potties at the same time. Some parents feel that you should allow no switching or you may have a tantrum on your hands.

- For twins who like doing EVERYTHING together, even after one or both can use the adult toilet, you may need to keep one potty chair in the bathroom awhile longer.

I think I deserve the reward for potty training twins. If one of them wasn't running to the bathroom, I was.

Robyn Neuman, Beaver Dam, WI

Separation from a Parent

If you have been the primary toilet trainer and anticipate being absent during part of the process, you should prepare your child and do some follow-up while you're gone.

- Suggest to the other parent or whoever will be carrying on the process that this book be required reading, at least mark significant passages. Prepare the person who will be in charge with tips and your observations on how best to handle things.

- Explain in simple language that you will be gone for a while, but that everything else will be the same (if it will; do prepare him or her for any changes you know about). Don't make a big deal of the absence. Promise to bring back something special for the child and then do it!

- Try to telephone while you're gone. Casually ask if your child has been going to the toilet as usual. If the answer is *"yes,"* express your delight. If the answer is *"no,"* tell the child you hope it will be *"yes"* the next time you call.

- If your child regresses when you return, don't show disappointment or promote shame.

Chapter 7

What If My Already-Trained Child Has Accidents?

❦

Becoming toilet trained is like learning to walk. It happens in fits and starts, two steps forward and one step back. Even among fully trained children, accidents can *(and often do)* happen. Occasional accidents are part of the toilet training process. Frequent accidents, however, may be an indicator that your child is not quite ready.

Moments of great excitement or fear, absorption in play, or a bad dream can be the cause of an occasional accident. Illness, stress of any kind, or jealousy of an infant sibling may bring on repeated accidents or even real regression.

Fear of using a strange toilet can be the reason behind an accident, with a child choosing the lesser of two evils.

Accidents

- Consider the possibility of an undiagnosed illness or an allergic reaction to certain foods or beverages (milk and milk products are often culprits), if your child has repeated unexplained accidents, or can't stay dry for two hours. Check with your doctor.

- If your child is ill, expect accidents until he or she has recovered enough to regain control.

- Don't punish a child for an accident. Clean up in a matter-of-fact way, help the child change clothes if necessary, and say no more about it.

- Use language like, *"I know you wanted to go in the potty but you just had an accident. Don't feel sad. You'll get better at this."*

- Don't be surprised if your child feels worse than you do about an accident. Your main job might be to console him or her. A child who's anxious to please may agonize over what he or she sees as "shameful" behavior. You might tell your child about one of your own early accidents, if you think it will help.

- Encourage the child to go to the potty after the accident "just to see if there's any more" (*there often is*).

- Don't allow siblings to tease a child for accidents.

I made a big deal out of the trip to the store with my 3-year-old when he indicated he wanted Superman pants and agreed that he would keep the underpants dry. He had a couple of accidents but he was really trying. The next day he had only one accident and after that, no more wet pants. He wet and had bowel movements in the toilet from then on. I have to add that my son is very stubborn and I didn't think toilet learning was going to be easy but it was.

Beverley McMillan, Scappoose, OR

Deliberate "Accidents"

Most children can't perform at will, but sometimes a child who is able to tries to punish or threaten a parent with this powerful weapon. *"Give me _____ or I'll _____ ..."* and *"Stop talking on the phone or I'll _____ ..."* are good attention getters.

- Don't overreact. This is not the time to give the attention that's so desperately desired.

- Do say that it's the child's ACT that disappoints you or makes you angry. (Be sure the child knows you still love him or her.)

- Don't rush to help the child get cleaned up. An already-trained child has learned to be uncomfortable in wet or soiled pants, and a little discomfort now may help to prevent repeat performances.

- Have the child help you clean the floor and rinse out his or her pants, and remember that an *especially* good job of handwashing will be required afterward. (A quick bathtub clean-up is sometimes needed too.)

- Enforcing the rule of clean clothing needs to be the parent's responsibility. Soiled clothing will require adult assistance while wet ones can usually be handled by a child alone.

Later, be sure your child gets plenty of love and attention, and be generous with praise for every example of good behavior.

> **I thought Eric would never quit having accidents. Finally on his 4th birthday he said, *"Mom, I'm 4 now and I'm not going to mess my pants any more."* And except for occasional night accidents, he hasn't!**
> *Jessica Murray, Ventura, CA*

Regression

Regression (*back to square one!*) may seem, at first to be simply a series of accidents, but it goes on . . . and on. It's more likely to have an emotional cause than a physical one, and it's most likely to occur during a period of stress: a new baby in the family, a death, separation from a parent. It may last for some time. If there is regression for any reason, lack of elimination control will probably be the first symptom.

- If regression is total and lasts more than a week or so, give up and go back to diapers.

- Realize that a jealous child is trying to compete with a new baby on its own level. Play up the boring and the unappealing aspects of infancy while stressing the advantages of being older.

- Casually suspend some "big-boy/big-girl" privileges—the later bedtime, some grown-up foods, certain television programs—and show surprise if the child complains. More important, do try to spend as much time as possible alone with the child.

- Try to get to the bottom of any other worry you suspect is a cause of regression. Help a child work through grief or explain a separation in terms the child can understand. Children often suffer from guilt when bad things happen, thinking they are to blame.

- Have your child help you clean up as much as is realistic, but don't shame or scold.

- Go back to toilet training when you think the child is ready for it (he or she may very well tell you), but don't make references to "the first time." This is a fresh start.

- Have someone else take over the major part of the retraining, if possible, to enhance the relief of that fresh start. And don't feel like a failure or a bad parent if you do this. In fact, you should be proud of yourself for recognizing a problem and doing something positive.

After spending one miserable week being involved with my 2½-year-old's accidents, I simply asked him if he still wanted to be in diapers. He said yes, and so he wore them for a few more weeks. Later, he came to me and said, *"Mommy, no more diapers."* I am beginning to learn that I do not want the power (not that you can ever have it) over my child's "self."

Mrs. B. Leckart, Los Angeles, CA

Regression may surface only for nighttime bed-wetting for the little older child. It can be a subconscious call for attention.

- Don't scold or call attention to a wet bed other than matter-of-factly changing the bedding. Calling a child a baby might be exactly what he or she wants to hear since it's the baby who is perceived as getting all the attention.

- Do call A LOT of attention to a dry bed.

- Try to put a new baby to bed first so you can focus on a relaxed bedtime with the older sibling.

- Allow a child who has begun wetting the bed again the choice of wearing a diaper at bedtime without any negative connotations, such as *"you must still be a baby."*

Chapter 8

How Can I Deal with Bed-Wetting?

❦

Bed-wetting is not considered to be a real problem (it's called *enuresis*) by most pediatric heath care providers until after a child is 5 or 6 years old. It may happen occasionally or every night. While it's distressing and frustrating for parents, you should bear in mind that a third of children over 3 and a quarter of those over 4 lack nighttime control. Even by ages 6 to 7, one child in seven wets while sleeping. Estimates are that five to seven million children wet their beds regularly. Small comfort—but at least you're not alone!

Remind yourself, every time you have to face a wet bed, that no child *wants* to be a bed-wetter. Your child's desire for nighttime control is probably greater than yours. It's been said by many, but it bears repeating:

A child should never be punished for wetting the bed.

Bed-wetting is not deliberate. It is less of a learned skill and more of a physiological development. Nighttime control is largely involuntary. Often control can be learned through behavior modification techniques alone or in conjunction with other help but often, even with help, patience is needed. For some children, just the body maturation of preadolesence removes the problem. It is said that 15% of bed-wetting children get over the problem without treatment each additional year as they mature.

Some Possible Causes for Bed-wetting

- Deep sleep may make it impossible for many children to respond to body signals. Some call it "arousal dysfunction" because you don't wake up to normal stimuli of a full bladder.

- Lack of awareness, even in a light sleeper.

- Heredity. If family members have been prone to bed-wetting, a child often is too. If one parent was a bed wetter then a child has a 50% chance of doing so. If both parents were, then there is a 75% chance that a child will be, too.

- Stress caused by changes in a child's life or illness.

- Constipation, which can inhibit bladder capacity. (See page 32.)

- Allergy to milk, which may be tested by removing all milk products from the child's diet for several weeks. (A calcium supplement may be recommended by your physician). Other food sensitivities may also be involved.

- Illness (especially if treated with drugs) during which usual nighttime control may be lost and not regained for some time after recovery.

- Urinary tract infections, especially if the child is a girl.

- Small bladder capacity and/or an irritable bladder is believed by some to be a cause for bed-wetting problems.

- Sickle-cell anemia, one symptom of which may be the inability to stay dry all night. (This disease is common in children of color.)

My husband and friends can't believe that I wet the bed until I was 11 but it's true. My sister did also until she was 10 and my brother until he was 7. I can remember all of those mornings waking up being spanked while I was still sleeping because I had wet the bed. At a physical, the doctor told my father to spank us because we were just too lazy to get up in the night. NOT TRUE. I never once felt the sensation of having to go to the bathroom while sleeping. I wish I knew who that doctor was. I'd give him a piece of my mind.

Elaine Arter, O'Fallon, MO

I have been living with this problem with my daughter who just turned 7 on and off for about 3 years. She had a full 18 months of being dry though I now believe it was probably because of the medicine she was taking for her bronchitis. We are working on this together now because she wants to be dry all the time. However, I have come to realize that parents can be too accepting which denies the child's desire to solve the problem. From what I've read 96% of children who wet when they sleep are simply DEEP SLEEPERS. The way to solve the problem is to break the deep sleep pattern. When we'd take her to the bathroom at night, we'd try to wake her—no zombie trips. Using an alarm belt, she was able to break the cycle in a few months and it's never been a problem since.

Teri Hay, Lancaster, PA

Helping Your Child, Psychologically Speaking

- Remember that punishing, scolding, and embarrassing a child have been proven NOT to help a child achieve nighttime control. Don't use these methods!

- Take your child to the doctor for a check-up just in case there's a physical cause for the bed-wetting. Seldom, however, is the problem physical. Still this will assure both you and the child that everything possible is being done.

- Be sure to tell your children that you know that they are not doing this on purpose, and that the problem doesn't make you love or admire them any less. Refer to them only as "accidents."

- Don't let siblings tease a child.

"Mom! Theron's dried his bed again."

- Explain to a son that bed-wetting is twice as common in boys than girls and that he is definitely not the only boy with this problem.

- Practice positive imaging. Help a child relax at bed-time and imagine waking up dry. Doctors are using this form of treatment with much success, especially with children 6 years and older. The audio-suggestion bedtime story tape, *Bedwetting* by Speigal & Associates *(206-232-9474)* may help in this area. Also try whispering encouraging words to your child while he or she is sleeping.

- Explain to your child, using simple language, that he or she is experiencing a maturational delay and that there is nothing seriously wrong. This problem is outgrown by 99% of the population. *(Don't mention that the "cure" often comes with the onset of puberty.)*

- Offer rewards for nighttime control as you have for daytime toilet training (see *Rewards,* page 51). The use of progress charts with stars or check marks is often a helpful motivator. Ask your child for ideas for rewards.

- Consider professional counseling if secondary enuresis occurs—that is bed-wetting by a child who has been considered nighttime trained (dry at night for four to six months) but begins to wet again. If a medical reason can't be found, it may be suggested that you look for a psychological one.

I assure my 5 and 8 year old that this won't go on forever and that they should think of their brain as a computer that has a short circuit to their bladder. Meanwhile their bodies are growing and someday their brain will make the connection and it will stop.

Chris Young, Fallbrook, CA

Practically Speaking

Not everyone agrees that all these ideas work, but for many they have.

- Work on bladder-stretching exercises. Have your child hold his or her urine during the day as long as possible. Starting and stopping the stream of urine may also increase muscle control.

- Have your child lie down on a bed in a sleeping position and "hold back" as long as possible before urinating. Practice at this will help a child learn to recognize body signals while lying down.

- Restricting fluid intake before bedtime, some believe will help; others feel it's best to have EXTRA fluids so bladder fullness is easier to notice. Certainly never let a child go to bed thirsty. Do avoid carbonated and caffeine drinks. Eliminate milk products after noontime, if you suspect or see a causal relationship. (Some children need to go off milk completely but don't do that for more than a few days without your doctor's supervision.)

- Be sure a child goes to the bathroom before going to bed.

- Make sure pajamas are easy to remove. Have extra ones easily available.

- Is the way to the bathroom lit? Night lights plugged in to all available outlets are an inexpensive investment.

- Wake your child up before YOU go to bed, taking him or her to the bathroom. It might help and should at least reduce some of the bladder's contents. Some feel, however, this fosters a dependency on parents that interferes with the task the child must learn alone.

- Consider checking out the other books on this topic such as *A Parent's Guide to Bed-Wetting Control* (Pocket Books) by Azrin and Besalel, which deals with the bell and pad method, or *Waking Up Dry: How to End Bedwetting Forever* (Writer's Digest) by M. Scharf, Ph.D. for more ideas. The book, *Dry All Night* by Alison Mack (Little Brown) has information for parents as well as a 4-color illustrated story for children encouraging self-charting, bladder exercises and creative visualization. Also for children are *All By Myself* by Anna Hines (Clarion/Houghton-Mifflin), and *Sammy the Elephant & Mr. Camel: A Story to Help Children Overcome Enuresis* by Mills and Crowley (Magination Press).

- Contact your local children's hospital, behavioral pediatics clinic or sleep disorder center, as many now offer enuresis counseling.

> For my 8-year-old who goes on sleepovers, we put a plastic sheet and a beach towel in the bottom of the sleeping bag which he fixes once he's there. Clean clothes are kept under his pillow. If he has wet, he gets dressed, and rolls it all up. The sleeping bag and all are washed when he gets home. He has not been embarrassed and had a great time he might have missed.
>
> *Chris Young, Fallbrook, CA*
>
> In our family, we have chosen to regard bed-wetting past 3 or 4 as a variation of normal development. Away from home, our 4½ year old wears special "nighttime dry pants." At home the bed is protected and in the morning we help him change if he is wet, and if he is dry, nothing much is said. The result is a child who is not worried about the issue. Of course, if and when he asks for help, I would do whatever I could to help him gain nighttime control.
>
> *Brooke Greene, Cloverdale, CA*

The Disposable Choice

Unfortunately bed-wetting is an inconvenience that must be dealt with. The choice boils down to doing laundry (bedding or cloth training pants) or using disposables (as a diaper/pant or a bed pad). Here are options and outlets for disposables. (See pages 40, 45 for cloth diaper information.)

In the regular outlets you should be able to find:

Pull-Ups Training Pants from Huggies.
Disposable pull-on diapers have a stretch ability as well as tear-away sides. Available in 3 sizes. Size *large* is for children 39 pounds to 59 pounds.

Walker 3
Available from Luvs and Pampers for children 26 pounds and up.

Big Boy/Big Girl Training Pants from Drypers Pull–up diapers available in *medium* and *large*.

When regular disposables no longer fit:

If your child outgrows standard disposables but not the need for them, look to these resources:

Youth Briefs
This is a small version of Attends for children 35 pounds to 70 pounds. Ask any supplier of Attends to order these for you if not stocked, or call HDIS, *800-538-1036*.

Attends Wrap Around Briefs
These side-tape disposables from Procter and Gamble come S *(20"–31")*, M *(32"–44")* and L *(45"–58")* as waist/hip measurements. Found in home medical supply stores if not elsewhere. For dealer information you can always contact: Procter and Gamble, PO Box 599, Cincinnati, OH 54201, *800-285-6064*. Home delivery is available from HDIS, *800-538-1036*.

DRIpride Ultra Disposable Briefs
These disposables come with double tape tabs
on each side and have a flexible leg gathers.
Sizes are based on waist/hip measurements,
S *(20"– 31")* M *(32"– 43")* L *(44"– 58")*. Available from
Direct Delivery Service, *800-659-8037.*

Ambeze Jr. Incontinent Pants
Disposable, tape-tab diapers that fit up to a 28"
waist. For a dealer near you, contact:
Whitestone Products, 40 Turner Place,
Piscataway, NJ 08854, *800-526-3567.*

Surety's Fitted Briefs, Depends Fitted Briefs
These are two additional brands similar to those
mentioned above that are available for home
delivery from HDIS, *800-538-1036.*

Tranquility Slimline
Disposable, side-taped closing, youth underpants
start for 35 pounds/18" to 28" waist/hips. Also a
cotton brief with high capacity disposable pad liners.
For a brochure or dealer near you call Principle Business Enterprises, Dunbridge, OI I 43414, *800-843-3385.*

If you prefer to use disposable underpads:

Disposable bedpad liners or underpads in approximate
30" to 36" squares can save a lot of laundry though they do
not come cheap. *Tuckables,* for instance, have side flaps that
tuck under the mattress to hold them in place. Some
supermarkets and drugstores carry some brands. You can
check your hospital supply store, or call these resouces for
ordering information or for a dealer in your area.

Direct Delivery Service *(DRIpride Underpads)*   *800-659-8037*
Paper-Pak Products *(Dri-Sheet, Supersorb)*   *800-635-4560*
Principle Business *(Tranquility Slimline Care Pads)* *800-843-3385*
Bruce Medical Supply *(Durasorbs)*   *800-225-8446*
HDIS *(Tuckables, Depends, Attends)*   *800-538-1036*

*(HDIS offers sample assortment packs of briefs and underpads so you
can decide which items will work best for you. Call for information.)*

The Battle of the Bedsheets

You can't make a child stop wetting the bed at night. Only the child can do it, and then only when the brain and bladder are willing. Many parents believe that a bed-wetter can and should be responsible for changing a wet bed and, perhaps, for laundering the sheets. They do this not to embarrass or punish the child, but for practical reasons. It is one way to teach a child that people are expected to clean up after themselves. For some it's been all the motivation they need but not for all. At any rate, the process of cleaning up—or keeping bedding dry—should be made as painless (for you *and* your child) and as efficient as possible.

- Make up a bed with two sets of bedding (including two rubber sheets) so only the top set needs to be stripped during the night. If fitted sheets are too hard for your child to manage, use flat sheets instead.

- Use an old waterproof crib sheet, plastic tablecloth, shower curtain or a large plastic garbage bag to protect the mattress if you don't have rubber sheets or a plastic mattress cover.

- Cover your sheets with a rubberized flannel pad like the pads you used for your baby. If a juvenile bedding store doesn't have it in a large size, check out a fabric store. They usually sell it by the yard.

- Buy a good plastic bed sheet from a medical supply store. They are light weight.

- Line the bed with a large bath towel tucked in sideways over a plastic protector. If the bed isn't too wet, the child can simply pull off the towel and go back to sleep.

- Don't forget to protect the pillow with a zippered plastic cover. Kids do move around a lot at night.

- Use one-piece washable coverlets to avoid the extra top sheet getting wet and you'll have one piece less to wash.

- Keep a sleeping bag nearby for a child to finish off a night's sleep if neither of you plan to change bedding.

- Keep an extra set of pajamas available and keep a plastic laundry basket or plastic bag handy for bed bedding.

- If you haven't protected your mattress well enough, sprinkle baking soda on the wet area. It absorbs the moisture, but more importantly, the odor. Urine doesn't contain bacteria, so just drying out blankets is okay unless you need to deal with odor.

- Encourage a child who wet to shower in the morning. The tell-tale odor of urine needs to be avoided.

- Be sure to have a sturdy washing machine.

I use *Nikky Dry Bed* pants on my 4½ year old who wets about half the time. These cotton underpants are thickly lined and very absorbant. These pants really do keep the bed dry. They are fairly expensive but they are easier to wash than a whole set of sheets.

Martha Sherman, Falls Church, VA

My 5 year old was a very sound sleeper and never woke at night. He wore a diaper and we never made an issue of it. We tried bladder training exercises suggested by the doctor but he got frustrated. Then I bought an alarm that attached to his underpants that went off at the first sign of dampness. Within a week he was dry all night.

Peggy Robinson-Wilson, Anchorage, AK

I'd double make the bed with one waterproof pad and a sheet, and a second pad and sheet on top. At night we could just strip off the wet layer—having dry ones underneath—and put her in dry pajamas.

Lois Patterson, Bloomington, WI

I discovered that using a bath rug with rubber backing to be excellent bed protection, especially when traveling with the kids. They come in various sizes and can easily rolled up and packed.

Cinda Elser, North Lima, OH

When my daughter was wetting her bed, I took her much loved Sesame Street sheets off. I told her they weren't going back on until she stopped wetting because Big Bird did not like to be all wet. She never wet again. (*I hope this works on my twin boys!*)

Rebecca Kerr, Chittenango, NY

Helpful Signaling Devices

In general, moisture alarms are not suggested for use until a child is 5 or 6 years old since a child needs to be cognitively involved and active in the program. The primary principle of these alarms is to awaken children while they are just starting to urinate. At first, a child probably will not wake up until the bladder is completely emptied. However, as conditioning progresses, a child begins to awaken at the first drop of wetness thus helping a child learn to wake up to the feeling of a full bladder.

The wet-sensitive alarm pad is giving way to smaller, less intrusive devices that clip on children's clothes or wrist with a wet-sensor cord that is attached to underwear. Often a bedpad alarm has to be saturated to respond, but those worn by a child are placed more strategically so they respond to the first sign of wetness, allowing a child to awaken before the bladder has completely emptied.

The disadvantages of the alarm are fairly obvious. The sound may upset the child (*though some children have been known to sleep through it*) and disrupt the household. Siblings may awaken, too—the last thing an embarrassed child wants to happen. You must be willing to get up when the alarm first sounds and wake your child if it wasn't heard. Alarms then have to be reset. On the plus side, alarms have a high success rate, with reports of 75% to 85% effectiveness in a week to a few months.

> I had a horrible bedwetting problem as a child. It was agonizing. When I was 7 or 8 my mother used an alarm system which was triggered by dampness and woke me up "just in time" every night. It was terrific! For the first time in my life I learned nighttime control (in less than a week) and I felt like a normal person! *Anonymous, Minneapolis, MN*

Cause for Alarm

These are some of the popular alarm devices on the market. There are alarms available through the Sears and J.C. Penny catalogs. Some medical supply companies or pharmaceutical departments will order one for you. Others are available by mail.

Wet-NO-More II
Travis International
100 Main-Sumner
Coos Bay, OR 97420
800-4-DRY BED
503-269-6969

A comfortable sensor attaches to a foam belt or underwear for males and females. No wires. Unlimited free 800 phone counseling covering the product program. For ages 5-9. Available by mail only for under $60. (Also available are wireless models from $185 to $325.)

SleepDry Alarm
StarChild/Labs
PO Box 404
Aptos, CA 95001
800-346-7283
408-662-2659

This system is available through pharmacies, doctors and bed-wetting clinics but can also be ordered direct for children 5 years or older. They offer a complete satisfaction guarantee as well as phone counseling. The product is the size of a small match box. It snaps on to clothes and the sensor is also non-instrusive. Under $50.

Wet-Stop
Palco Labs
8030 Soquel Ave
Santa Cruz, CA 95062
800-346-4488
408-476-3151

The Wet-Stop is similarly small in size to the SleepDry Alarm but differs in attachment systems. The essential difference is a soft cotton pad for the underwear which is attached to the urine sensor with Velcro. They offer a guarantee of success within 12 months. The price is $55.

Potty Pager
1285 N. Cedarbrook
Boulder, CO 80304
800-497-6573
303-440-8517

This small alarm that is inserted in underpants (no wires) does not buzz but vibrates in an on/off cycle to awaken a child after moisture activates it. Under $50.

Nytone Enuretic Alarm
Nytone Medical Products
2424 South 900 West
Salt Lake City, UT 84119
801-973-4090

The small alarm attaches to the wrist with a moisture sensor that clips to the outside of underpants. Telephone consultation available. Available in pharmacies, home healthcare stores, and by mail. Suggested retail price under $50.

Wee-Alert
Health Guardian
1112 7th Ave
Monroe, WI 53566
608-328-8947

This pad is placed under the sheet and attaches to an alarm at bedside. Sold by Sears. Suggested retail price under $65. (Also available with a light that shines in the eyes for under $85.)

Several companies offer conditioning devices for bedwetters with counseling. The fees are not low but they work with you and don't leave you alone with alarm devices because they feel that support and proper use is the key to success.

ERD (*Enuresis Research and Development*)
578 Grand Ave
St. Paul, MN 55102
612-221-9787

This service offers one-on-one counseling that is individually designed with a behavior modification program that includes an alarm. There are programs at three price points that range from $300 to $995. Their service claims a success rate of more than 90%.

Pacific International, LTD
555 Birch Street
Nekoosa, WI 54457
800-447-2233
715-886-4550

This company has been around many years and advertises widely. The alarm system they loan you, is made by them and contracted with you through a consultant. When finished, the system must be returned. If used with a second child, the cost is 50% of the original fee. The cost is not low and prices are not given over the phone.

Drug Therapy for Helping the Bed-wetter

Drug therapy can be effective but should be reserved for children past the age of 6 and be discussed, prescribed and monitored by your child's pediatric heath care provider. It seems to work for some children but not for others. Drugs offer quick results, but once stopped, a large percentage of children return to bed-wetting. Some parents and professionals discourage the use of these measures, especially if they are chosen just because they're easy.

Imipramine (*aka* Tofranil, SK-Pramine, Janimine, or Imavate), has been commonly used to treat bedwetting for many years but it is not recommended by the American Academy of Pediatrics. It is a toxic drug and antidepressant that can cause personality changes and lethargy. If used, it must be closely monitored.

Another drug you may have heard mentioned is oxybutinin (*aka* Ditropan) which is really not used for bedwetting but only for those with proven bladder instability as reflected in daytime incontinence. It might be used with adults, but not children.

The current popular perscription drug (popular in large part to the advertising campaign by the drug company, Rhône-Poulenc Rorer) recently approved for enuresis treatment is desmopressin acetate (*aka* DDAVP), a synthetic version of the anti-diuretic hormone, ADH. This suppresses the kidneys from making urine which some question as a viable therapy by creating this temporary, artifical response. It comes as a nasal spray and with a VERY high price tag. It is not to be used by those with cystic fibrosis, nasal polyps, epilepsy, heart or kidney disease. Some doctors like to use it because of its fast effect for success; others like it for the short term to get a jump start on successes when used in conjunction with other methods. Relapse rates after use is discontinued is high.

- Remember that any drug can be lethal in the wrong hands. If you are using a drug to treat your child's bed-wetting, be sure it is stored safely out of the child's reach, and away from siblings too. Children have died from overdoses of these drugs.

- Drugs and alarm devices are sometimes used together to treat enuresis. Again, ask your doctor (or some other professional) and use common sense to help you decide what's best for your child.

- Try to keep the problem in perspective. You and your child should decide for yourselves (with advice from caring professionals) which is best for your situation.

One Last Therapy

While I admit my bias prevents me from encouraging this last therapy, I would be wrong not to mention it for those who wish to pursue this route. Many chiropractors treat bed-wetting through spinal adjustments and many families have found (according to a *Dear Abby* column) success at their hands. But there is nothing that even chiropractors can point to in their own literature with controlled studies giving statistical validity (*and studies have been done*) to this premise despite testimonial evidence of success.

National Enuresis Society

This association was formed in 1992 to disseminate information to parents and professionals advising them of methods to help children overcome this problem rather than just waiting until it is outgrown. For information, contact:

NES, P.O. Box 6351, Parsippany, NJ 07054.

Company references

Americare Products
3950A Nebraska Street
Newportville, PA 19056
800-220-CARE

Baby Motivations Co.
9706 Sugar Tree Court
Houston, TX 77070
800-421-4338

Baby Bjorn
PO Box 70035
Marietta, GO 30007
800-593-5522
404-565-5522

Brite-Times/Inflate-a-Potty
15237 Sunset Blvd #91
Pacific Palisades, CA 90272
800-933-6340

Century Products
9600 Valley View Road
Macedonia, OH 44056
800-837-4044
216-468-2000

Children On The Go
1670 South Wolf Road
Wheeling, IL 60090
800-537-COTG
708-537-3797

Cosco Inc.
2525 State Street
Columbus, IN 47201
812-372-0141

Evenflo
1801 Commerce Drive
Piqua, OH 45356
800-233-5921
513-773-3971

First Years
One Kidde Drive
Avon, MA 02322
617-588-1220

Fisher-Price
636 Girard Avenue
East Aurora, NY 14052
800-432-5437

G.W. Dmka/Best Days
168 East Main Street
Prospect Park, NJ 07508
201-595-5599

Gerry Baby Products
12520 Grant Drive
Denver, CO 80241
800-456-2989

Innovative Distributing
19-910 Mainland Street
Vancouver, BC V6B-1A9
Canada
USA 1-800-9276923
Can. 604-681-4906

Little Tikes Co.
PO Box 2277
Hudson, OH 44236
800-321-0183

Little White House
13987 Carriage Road
Poway, CA 92064
619-748-9255

Mommy's Helper
PO Box 780838
Witchita, KS 67278-0838
316-636-9512

Michael Friedman Corp.
650 Fountain Avenue
Brooklyn, NY 11208
800-431-3166
718-257-7800

Nu-Line Industries
PO Box 217
214 Nu-Line Street
Suring, WI 54174
800-456-2989

Pelican Company
1914 B Street
Marysville, CA 95901
916-741-2317

Playskool Baby
108 Fairview Court
Northvale, NJ 07647
800-752-9755
201-767-0900

Primex Co.
19422 Coralwood Lane
Huntington Beach, CA 92646
714-962-9790

Safety 1st
210 Boylston Street
Chestnut Hill, MA 02167
800-962-7233

Sassy
1534 College S.E.
Grand Rapids, MI 49507
616-243-0767

Shades of Jade
720 Fessey Park Road
Nashville, TN 37204
615-298-4056

Mail order companies carrying potty seats and diapers

	customer service	to order
After the Stork	505-243-9100	800-333-5437
Baby Bunz & Co.	707-829-5347	800-767-4559
Babyworks	503-645-4349	800-422-2910
Biobottoms	707-778-7168	800-766-1254
Hand in Hand	800-872-3841	800-872-9745
Livonia Catalog	704-697-5811	800-543-8566
Natural Baby Co.	609-737-2895	800-388-BABY
One Step Ahead	708-615-2110	800-274-8440
Practical Parenting	612-475-3527	800-255-3379
Right Start Catalog	818-707-7100	800-548-8531
R. Duck Company	805-964-4343	800-422-3825
Sensational Beginnings	313-242-2147	800-444-2147
TL Care	415-626-3127	415-626-3127

INDEX

Books by Vicki Lansky...

- Feed Me I'm Yours
- The Taming of the CANDY Monster
- Fat-Proofing Your Child
- Practical Parenting Tips Yrs.1–5
- Toilet Training
- KoKo Bear's New Potty
- Birthday Parties
- Welcoming Your Second Baby
- A New Baby at KoKo Bear's House
- KoKo Bear's Big Earache
- Getting Your Child to Sleep... and Back to Sleep
- Trouble-Free Travel with Children
- Baby Proofing Basics   • Dear Babysitter Handbook
- Divorce Book for Parents   • 101 Ways to Tell Your Child I Love You   • 101 Ways to Make Your Child Feel Special   • 101 Ways to Say I Love You (for adults)
- 101 Ways to be a Special Dad   • Kids Cooking
- Microwave Cooking for Kids   • Games Babies Play
- ANOTHER USE FOR...101 Common Household Items

For a free mail order catalog listing all her books or to order any, call 1-800-255-3379 or write to Practical Parenting, Dept TT, Deephaven, MN 55391. Also to order (MC/VISA) this:

Folding Potty Seat Adapter
(featured on page 23)
$9.95 plus $2.25 postage/hdlg